365

Bedtime Stories

Translated from the French
by Maureen Spurgeon

Brown Watson
ENGLAND

1 January

Happy New Year!

Last night, it was New Year's Eve. We had a lovely party at our house to celebrate! Mummy cooked a gorgeous meal with a really mouth-watering pudding for afters! Then Daddy put on some records and we threw streamers and had lots of fun.

At midnight, we lit sparklers to greet the New Year and Uncle Felix called all the children together and gave us some mistletoe.

Guess what we did then? Well, we tip-toed across the room like Red Indians and gave a bunch to our Mummy! I'm sure I could see a few tears in Mummy's eyes when we gave her the mistletoe.

My eyes felt a bit prickly, too – but that was only because of the smoke from the sparklers.

We were up until three o'clock in the morning! In the end, I was glad to slide into bed and close my eyes! It was eleven o'clock this morning before any of us got up!

After we had washed and dressed, we went to wish Mummy and Daddy a Happy New Year. Then we went and greeted all our friends.

My wish for the New Year is that men will stop fighting and going to war. Happy New Year, everyone!

2 January

Tom Thumb

There was once a woodcutter who was too poor even to feed his seven sons. "Tomorrow," he said to his wife, "we shall have to take the boys and leave them in the forest. Some rich hunter is bound to find them!"

Now, Tom Thumb, the youngest of his seven sons, heard everything. Next day, before setting off, he filled his pockets with white pebbles, dropping them one by one along the way. So, when the woodcutter left the boys, Tom Thumb was able to lead his brothers back home!

But a few days later, the woodcutter took them to the forest again – and this time, Tom Thumb had no pebbles to help them find the way back. They were well and truly lost!

3 January

They started to walk, not really knowing where they were going. But after a while, they came to a big castle, the home of a giant who had seven daughters. He said the brothers could stay the night – but only because he planned to eat them the next morning!

Now, his seven daughters slept all together in a big bed, each one with a crown on her head.

During the night, Tom Thumb took the crowns and put them on his brothers' heads.

4 January

The giant was about to eat the seven boys, but the crowns made him think they were his daughters! So, he went into the other room. Not stopping to look, he ate the seven girls instead! As the giant slept after eating so much, Tom took his seven-league boots and put them on. Whoever wore them could travel far at great speed, and so he was able to lead the way home.

As word spread, noblemen gave Tom their important messages to deliver. Tom Thumb soon became rich, and his family were never in want again.

5 January

The Story of the Epiphany

Long, long ago, in a country called Palestine, three wise men, who were also kings, were following a bright star. They knew that this star was the sign that the Son of God had been born, and they had travelled many miles to give Him gifts of gold, frankincense and myrrh.

At last, the star stopped – above the roof of a humble stable.

"The Child must be there," breathed the first king, Balthazar.

"Here?" said Melchior, the second.

6 January

"It's only a stable!" said Melchior. "We shall go inside," decided Caspar, the third king.
And there, with the ox and the ass, they saw the Child whom they had been seeking. "Your Son is the Saviour of the World – Christ, our New-Born King," Melchior told Mary and Joseph. The three wise men knelt at the manger where Baby Jesus lay.
"Today," said Caspar, "is a day of rejoicing for us."
And now, Christians call it the Day of the Epiphany.

7 January

Warning! Do Not Disturb!

To escape the winter weather, many animals fall into a deep sleep. We call it hibernating. Pets which hibernate, such as tortoises, are best kept in the attic or a shed, somewhere nice and dry. Hedgehogs like to roll into a ball and snuggle down deep in straw. Hibernating animals may seem barely alive. Nothing will wake them until springtime, and they will not feel hungry or thirsty, either. Think how lucky they are, sleeping the winter away!

8 January

The bear sleeps all winter, too. When he has eaten all that he wants, he snuggles down right inside a nice, cosy hole. With his warm fur and thick layer of fat, there is no danger of him becoming cold!

The winter ermine does not hibernate, but this little animal is very smart! In summer, the ermine is brown. But in winter, it has the most beautiful coat of white fur, all except for the black tip of its tail. This is so that the ermine can hide itself from its enemies against the white background of snow.

9 January

Not a Good Idea....

Matthew is a clever boy, but he does not like working hard. Instead, he likes finding short cuts and thinking up ways to make life easy!

For instance, one day, he was out with his little sister. She wanted a ride on the sledge, but Matthew was not going to pull her along. Oh, no! He wanted a ride, too! So, he threaded a long cord through the collar of Mowgli, his next-door neighbour's dog, who he was supposed to be taking for a walk.....

10 January

To keep Mowgli still, Matthew gave him a whole bag of popcorn which his mother had made.

"Now, let's go!" he told the big dog, pleased when Mowgli started off at quite a pace.

All went well when they kept in a straight line – but at the first bend.... disaster! The cord broke and Matthew and his sister were thrown to the ground.

Poor Matthew! He was the one who had to pull the sledge and his sister all the way home, after all – not Mowgli!

11 January

Good-Hearted Freddie

It was Freddie's eleventh birthday. His Mum and Dad gave him the money to buy a personal stereo, plus a cassette recording of his favourite singer. No wonder he was smiling as he got to the shop!

"Hello, Freddie!" came a little voice behind him. Freddie turned round to see Mark, a boy from school. "It's my birthday!" Freddie told him, showing him the money. "I'm going to buy a personal stereo, and——"

12 January

"I was twelve yesterday," said Mark.
"But I didn't get anything....."
Freddie's heart began beating a little faster. He looked at his friend, not knowing quite what to say.
"We'll share the money if you like," he said at last. "Look, let's buy two pairs of basketball shoes! Right?"
"Freddie," said Mark, rather timidly, "you are a good friend. But what will your Mum and Dad say?"
Mark need not have worried. Freddie's parents were proud to think their son had such a kind heart.

13 January

The Hobby-Horse

Winter can be great fun when there is snow around! Peter and Laura always love every minute of it. They make slides, build great big snowmen and get their toboggan out.
But often it is cold, even when there is no snow! That is when Peter and Laura do something else – something which you could do, too.
Did you know that some old woollen socks or gloves can be great things to play with?
See if you can find an old sock that nobody wants...

14 January

Stuff the sock with scraps of cloth, wool or foam rubber chips, until it feels quite firm. Then push a broom handle or stick up to the heel, tying string or wool around the bottom of the sock and knotting it firmly to keep the wood in place. All you have to do then is to find some odd bits of wool or string to make a mane, sew on two buttons or circles of felt for eyes – and you have a lovely hobby-horse, ready for you to gallop around!

You can make puppets in much the same way, too. Why not have a try?

15 January

Winter Help for the Birds

Why not help birds in winter by making a bird feeder? Spread paste or glue over a plastic bottle, cover with pieces of bark or moss and leave to dry. Fill with nuts or bird-seed (bought cheaply from pet shops). Tie some thread through the bark or moss and hang up with the neck of the bottle facing downwards. Firmly packed, food will not come out of the bottle and the birds will enjoy getting food from inside. Any stray bits will soon be pecked up, anyway!

16 January

You will soon see how quickly the birds come to feed!

As well as nuts and bird seed, you will find that tits love berries and bits of fat, whilst sparrows like breadcrumbs. You can also give them water to drink, but be careful it does not freeze. To stop ice forming, just add one or two drops of cooking oil. You can also make a nesting-box. A big flower pot will do! Remember to put both the bird-feeder and the nesting-box not too near the house, and – most important – out of the sun.

17 January

Tracks and Trails

One winter's day, Jack and Lucy went out with their parents, following the tracks of animals in the snow.

"A rabbit's been along here!" cried Jack, pointing. "And this is where a hare has been jumping around!"

Lucy found some tracks left by the small feet of birds on the river bank.

"Ducks made these little triangles with their webbed feet," Jack told her. "And that's where a blackbird has been. His tracks are all the same size and the same distance apart."

18 January

Watch Out for the Dark!

"Hurrah!" cried Marian. "A bit of sunshine!" It seemed such a long time since she had felt the sun on her face, so she was very pleased.

Marian was also rather silly... She was so happy to see what a nice day it was, that she went into the garden without a coat – not a very sensible thing to do in winter-time!

Not only that, she decided to go for a walk in the woodland at the back of her home.

"Walkies, Bruce!" she called to next-door's dog. "Do you want to come with me?"

Bruce gave such an eager bark that she could not resist taking him along. The dog was always good company on a walk. Which was just as well – because Marian did not have much sense of direction......

19 January

It all seemed so clean and smelt so fresh in the woods! And with so much space to herself, Marian could practice her favourite gym exercises, enjoying herself so much that she had no idea how long she had been away from home! Nor did she remember how short the days are in winter. It was only when she began feeling hungry that she noticed how dark it was. "How can I find my way back?" she cried, very frightened. How glad she was then that she had Bruce with her! Otherwise, she would never have found her way home. Silly Marian!

20 January

21 January

Joel crossed over and grabbed the umbrella. Then he picked up the oranges and put them in her basket.
"Oh, thank you!" she cried.
"That's all right, lady!" smiled Joel.
"You know," she smiled back, "all my friends call me Poppy!"
"That old lady," said Tony as they walked on, "did she give you anything?"
"Oh, yes!" grinned Joel.
"How much?" asked Mark.
"She gave me a smile," said Joel simply. "And that was enough for me!"

Only a Smile ....

Mrs. Pope came shuffling along with the tiny steps of an old, old lady. Everyone in the neighbourhood called her Poppy, and whenever she heard that, she smiled. And as she smiled, her cheeks puffed out, so red and so round that people could hardly see her eyes. One rather windy morning, Poppy was coming back from market, a basket on one arm and holding an umbrella in her other hand.
"What a day!" thought the old lady. Suddenly, a gust of wind blew the umbrella from her hand – and just as poor old Poppy tried to get it, her basket burst open and oranges began rolling around on the pavement! Joel and his friends were on the opposite side of the road. When they saw what had happened, everyone burst out laughing – all except Joel.

The Blue Tit

Mimi, the pretty little Blue Tit, had just put on her scarf and her hat, ready to go out and find something to eat, when there was a sudden fall of snow. "Now, what shall I do?" she murmured, her beak chattering.

"See that farm?" said the birch tree. "Go into the barn and you will be nice and warm."

"And what will you do?" asked Mimi.

"Oh," laughed the birch tree, "I am used to this! Now, hurry along out of the cold!"

Mimi found that there were lots of other birds inside, busy pecking at the pig trough.

"Look who's come to join us!" said one of the birds. "Chippy the pig is sharing his food with us, Mimi! We shall eat well this winter, thanks to him!"

22 January

Oranges

It may be winter-time in Europe, but on the other side of the world, it's the orange-picking season! And there are lots of different things you can do with oranges.....

For instance, did you know that the head of a pin placed eight metres away from an orange is almost an exact scale model of the earth's size and distance away from the sun? When you next eat an orange, try cutting it in half and scoop out the flesh. Then, with the halves of peel, you can make pretty little lamps, just by putting a few drops of cooking oil in the bottom and using the white pith in the centre as a wick. Make sure you get an adult to help you, though, won't you.

23 January

24 January

Here is a recipe to make fresh orange lollipops! You need 12 lollipop or cocktail sticks, a length of kitchen foil, 15 teaspoons of caster sugar and the juice of one orange. Lightly oil the foil and lay the sticks across. Then dissolve the sugar in the orange juice over a gentle heat and stir. ASK A GROWN-UP TO HELP YOU! Test by dropping a tiny bit into a glass of water. When it "crystallises" (goes solid) in a few seconds, it is time to put a little on to the sticks. Leave to harden in a cool place or put in a refrigerator.

25 January

Ice and Snow

How much snow is there outside your home today? Several centimetres? Just a thin film? Or none at all? Because of the air which it traps inside, snow makes an excellent shelter and lining. Eskimo people use it as protection against the cold, as well as building their igloos with it, and lots of animals are sheltered by snow. Many hibernating insects would never survive the cold weather without a soft blanket of snow to cover them.

26 January

When the temperature falls to zero Celsius, the water on ponds and lakes becomes ice. But although it is very tempting to go skating, there is no telling whether or not the ice will hold. So often, outdoor skaters have fallen into icy water and been unable to surface because of the frozen ice covering the rest of the pond. Ducks, too, when they feel the icy weather coming, go flapping around trying to break the ice and get to the water. Then they have to fly towards the rivers where the water does not freeze over so easily.

27 January

The Wolf and the Seven Little Kids

There were once seven little kids who lived with their mother, a fine nanny goat. The only time she left them on their own was when she went shopping. "Be sure not to open the door while I'm out!" she would say. One day, the big, bad wolf heard her. And, as soon as Mother Goat had gone, he went to the house of the seven little kids and knocked at the door....

28 January

The seven little kids remembered what Mother Goat had said and did not open the door. Soon, the wolf came back with a box of sugared almonds he had bought at the sweet shop.
"If it's you, Mother Goat," one of the seven little kids cried out, "then show us your white paw!"
So the wolf went to the miller and asked him to whiten his right foot with flour. Then he went back to the seven little kids. Seeing the white paw, they thought it must be Mother Goat. So, they opened the door. And that wicked wolf leapt towards the seven little kids, gobbling up each one! When Mother Goat returned, she found her house was all topsy-turvy and the kids gone – all except the eldest one, who had hidden in the big grandfather clock. He told Mother Goat all that had happened. But, whatever could she do?

29 January

They soon found the wolf, following the sound of his snores, fast asleep after his big meal. Mother Goat took out her scissors, a big needle and some thread. And the moment she cut open the wolf's tummy, out jumped the six little kids! Then Mother Goat filled the wolf with pebbles and sewed him up! When he awoke, the stones made him feel so thirsty that he decided to have a drink. But the stones also made him so heavy that he fell into the well! How glad all the animals were to know they had seen the last of him!

30 January

The Ant and the Grasshopper

A grasshopper had spent the whole of the summer singing day and night. Then autumn had come, with the nights becoming colder. All too soon, winter followed, with the north wind blowing without stopping and ice everywhere. The grasshopper had done nothing to prepare for all this. Now, she was hungry and her store cupboards were empty. It was then that she remembered the little ant who had lived nearby. The whole summer through, this ant had worked steadily to get a store of food whilst the weather was fine, so that she would have a store of good things to eat. Just thinking about it now made the grasshopper's mouth water. Dare she call on the hardworking ant?

31 January

Without stopping to think twice, the grasshopper went and knocked at the ant's front door. Could she spare some food, just enough to eat until the spring? The grasshopper would pay back the ant without fail next August!
"I'm afraid not!" said the ant very firmly. "What did you do all summer long?"
"Well," replied the grasshopper, "I -I sang....."
"You sang," said the ant, "whilst I worked hard. Well now, you can dance!" And she closed the door.

1 February

Winter Games

It had been snowing all through the night. No wonder the children did not want to go to school next morning! "You will have time to go out and play after school!" said their teacher. "I am not giving you any homework today!" So, after school, the children began building the most enormous snowman. But David, the youngest, wanted to go sledging.

"You can't go by yourself!" said Mother. But the naughty little boy was soon on his sledge, going faster and faster downhill!

"How do I stop?" he shouted, tugging the guide-rope this way and that.

"Watch out!" yelled Roger, and the other children jumped out of the way just in time.

2 February

David and his sledge smashed right into that lovely, big snowman. It fell to pieces!

"Oh, no!" cried Bernard.

"After all our hard work!" cried Vicky, shaking her head.

"Mummy said you weren't to take out the sledge," scowled Patrick.

"All right, that's enough!" said Michael, the eldest. "This accident will teach David a lesson, believe me!"

And they all set to work again. But this time, David was there, helping to build another great big snowman.

3 February

Fun with Words

Sally-Anne was usually quite a chatterbox! So it was very strange when nobody heard her talking....

"What's wrong, Sally-Anne?" asked her sister, Cindy. "It's horrible outside," said Sally-Anne, "and there's nothing to do!"

"What about a word game?" smiled Cindy. "You guess one word, then a second. Join them up and they make another word. Listen and you'll see!"

"Now," Cindy went on, "my first word is not the truth...."

"Lie!" said Sally-Anne at once.

"And the second," said Cindy, "is the opposite to off!"

"On!" said Sally-Anne.

"Put the words together and you have a jungle animal," laughed Cindy. "Do you know what it is?"

4 February

"Lie.. on... Lion!" cried Sally-Anne. "Let's have another go!" "All right!" smiled Cindy. "My first is another word for happy. We often use it before the word Christmas.."

"Happy Christmas.." said Sally-Anne.

"No, Merry Christmas! The word is merry."

"Right! And the second is the opposite of come."

"Go!"

"Next, the shape of a ball."

"Round!" cried Sally-Anne. "So, the whole word is Merry-Go-Round! Can I think of the next word in the game?"

5 February

How Quiet It Is!

"Croak! Croak! Croak!" The harsh cries of the crows were the only sounds to be heard across the frozen stretch of land. Everything else was still and silent, in the grip of the cold weather.

"Croak! Croak!" cried one crow again. "What about this heap of compost? There are bound to be plenty of worms and maggots here, all good to eat!"

And with her friends, she pecked busily, scratching the compost heap with her claws.

"It's best if we eat as much as we can!" said another crow. "The sky is grey and I think it is going to snow. What shall we find to eat, then?"

"Perhaps," said another, "we can find something on the farms…"

6 February

"I don't think so!" objected the first crow. "Last time I set foot in a farmyard, I was attacked by the cockerel! No, we shall do better in the gardens."

And as the hours passed, so the crows gathered together, preparing to settle down for the night. Some were on the top of an old tower, others in trees. But what a noise there was! No longer was there silence, with the birds chattering and squawking until quite late in the evening. Then, after one last flight around the black sky, darkness fell. All was quiet again.

7 February

Does, Stags, Fawns and Roe Deer

In woods and forests, wild animals get very hungry in winter. They cannot find anything to eat because of the covering of snow. Nor are there any leaves on the trees.

A herd of Mother Deer – or Does – and their fawns will go for miles in search of food.

Luckily for some, forest rangers will put mangers out for them to feed each morning. The rangers fill them with bundles of straw and hay, and leave blocks of salt for the whole herd to lick.

The father deer, or stag, looks majestically on his family. Can you see the big antlers on his head? He will lose those when spring comes.

8 February

When he is old enough, a male fawn will leave the herd to live alone. And do not mix up the doe with the Roe Deer! The doe is the female of the stag – whereas the Roe Deer is a smaller type of deer and lives near grassland and meadows. Roe Deer like to eat young shoots and berries. You can pick them out by a white patch on their backs between their rear legs, and, above all, by the way they leap around. If you want to see it in the wild, be careful not to make a sound. Roe Deer are easily frightened.

9 February

How Vegetables Grow!

For once, there was no early morning frost, so Ian put on his jacket and walked over to the common, hoping to meet his friends.

The only person around was old Mr. Perryman. He had just finished pulling up the last few vegetables on his allotment.

"You're looking a bit sad!" Ian remarked to the old gentleman.

"Yes," sighed Mr. Perryman. "Because we will not be able to use this ground for much longer. A new building will be going up here very soon!"

"That's not right!" cried Ian. "What will happen to the little dwarfs you told me about, the ones who weave the roots and mould the vegetables under the ground?"

10 February

Ian was so worried about the news, he could hardly sleep that night. Early next morning, he got on his bike and went to the common again. A huge digger was already at work and Ian watched the big hole being dug in the earth.

There was no sign of any dwarfs. Ian could not understand it.

On the way back home, he met the greengrocer and told him about it.

"I shall explain to you how vegetables are really grown!" the man said. "It's really just as exciting as any story about dwarfs, you know!"

11 February

The Bear and the Two Friends

There were once two poor friends who decided to try and change their luck. They thought of the silliest ideas to do this – and the silliest of all is what they decided – which was to sell the splendid fur of a great bear to a fur dealer. The only thing was, the bear they had in mind was very much alive, running around the mountain! Capturing him would be quite a task for anyone.

Well, one fine morning, the two men set off to find the bear. They saw him much sooner than they expected, coming up behind them on his giant legs, lips parted in a fierce growl. Full of fear, the two would-be hunters fled. The first jumped up into the first tree he could find. The second stumbled on a stone and fell down....

12 February

Too frightened to move an inch, the man lay quite still, pretending to be dead.

Soon, the bear came up to the man and sniffed him, then went away. When he was quite sure that it was safe, his friend ran up to him. "Do you know," said the first man, "that bear spoke to me!"

"What did he say?" asked the second.

"Never sell a bear skin without first killing the bear!" came the reply. And, feeling even sillier than they ever had before, the two sillies went back to their village.

13 February

St. Valentine's Day, Tomorrow!

This evening, Daddy came back from his office with a big parcel.

"It's for Mummy!" he told us in a whisper. "A St. Valentine's Day present for tomorrow! But don't forget, it's to be a surprise!"

Now, this morning at breakfast, Daddy had winked across at us and said to Mummy, "Oh, blow it! I'd completely forgotten it's Valentine's Day tomorrow! Never mind dear, I'll make it up to you next year!"

Mummy did not say anything. But we could see she was not very pleased. We just ate our cornflakes and smiled across at each other.

We could not help wondering what would happen tomorrow....

14 February

This morning, Daddy came in the kitchen and put the parcel on the table. "Happy Valentine's Day, dear!" he said. Mummy pretended to be cross.

"You caught me out, you horror!" she said. "And I suppose these two little rascals were in on the secret!"

"But, what is St. Valentine's Day?" asked my little sister.

"It's the day for people who love each other," I said, "like Mummy and Daddy!"

As for that parcel – you will have to guess what was inside!

15 February

Puss-in-Boots

There was once a poor miller who had three sons. When he died, the eldest son was left his mill, the second son his donkey.... And the third and youngest son? He only got a cat.

"You may be a cat," the miller's son said, "but to me, you are my friend!" To his great surprise, the cat answered him.

"Bring me a pair of boots to wear and I shall make your fortune, master!" he said. So, that is what the miller's son did.

One day, when the cat was out hunting, he chanced to see the royal coach carrying the king and the princess. Out ran Puss-in-Boots, lifting a paw to make the coach stop.

16 February

"Sire," said Puss with a bow, "my master, the Marquis of Carabas, will be pleased to receive you at his castle!"

The king was very surprised and amused by this walking, talking cat – especially when Puss-in-Boots told him how rich his master was. And when they came to a splendid castle, Puss-in-Boots went in alone. He knew it was owned by a giant with special, magic powers. But Puss-in-Boots told the giant that he was sure such a huge man could never turn himself into a little animal, magic or no magic.....

17  February

This made the giant so angry, he changed himself into a mouse – which Puss-in-Boots ate in a single gulp! Very soon, the king and the princess were welcomed into the fine castle, with the miller's son, now dressed in some fine clothes, greeting them. The princess fell in love with him instantly, and the king was so delighted that he gave his daughter's hand to this charming, young nobleman, so handsome and so wealthy!

As for Puss-in-Boots, he lived many years as his master's loyal servant.

18 February

A Lovely Prize!

Joe is a boy who just loves animals. But his parents will not allow him to keep one in the house.

"It takes a lot of work to train and keep a pet," his mother always says. But today is the day of the Prize Draw at School. And Joe picks out a winning number, with a sweet little tabby kitten as his prize! He is so happy that his mother and father have to change their minds!

"I'll look after the kitten myself!" Joe promises. And, he will.

19 February

Surprises and Disguises!

Clothes.... lanterns.... hats.... streamers... there's always lots to do for the Mardi Gras carnivals held in many countries on Shrove Tuesday! And whether or not you celebrate Mardi Gras, here are a few fancy dress ideas you could try.

A dustbin bag with holes cut at the top and at both sides for your head and arms, is the perfect cloak for a witch or wizard – especially with a crooked carrot nose, pointed hat and a broom! Or how about using some coloured paper carrier-bags to make animal masks? Try slitting one down the sides first, to make two pieces. Then make four holes for eyes, nose and mouth, and gather up the two top corners and tie each with thread for two ears!

20 February

Do you have lots of imagination? Of course, you do! So, why not make a monster disguise, sticking cut-out face pieces on a paper carrier-bag mask? Try cutting out long, pointed cardboard nails to stick on to a pair of old rubber gloves to make vampire hands. And even household objects can give you plenty of ideas, too. A colander makes a splendid helmet, a frying pan a fine shield, and a biscuit tin a tomtom. Or what about a feather duster to use as an Indian head-dress? You're sure to have lots more ideas!

21 February

The Hare, the Rabbit and the Wild Boar

Neither Jo-Jo, the hare, nor Toto, the rabbit, had eaten very much for quite a long time. No shoots to nibble at, no fresh greens, nothing.... no matter how hard they searched. Worse still..... brrr! It was bitterly cold!

No wonder they both flapped their long ears down over their backs, trying to keep warm! But the best way they found to beat the cold was by running. The hare was a champion runner, reaching speeds of up to 60 kilometres an hour!

A hare's home is called a "form", and is a simple hole in the ground or under some bushes. The rabbit is a smaller animal. He digs a "warren" in the ground, where he lives with his doe – the mother rabbit – and their babies.

22 February

Oink, oink, oink! What a racket! That's because a family of wild boars are digging into the ground.

There may not be anything very much to eat close at hand, but the wild boar does not give up. Along with his sow and the baby boars, he will go for miles in search of roots, worms and insects.

But, beware! Wild boar can be very fierce, so it is best not to disturb them at all. The male wild boar has two long tusks which can cut like daggers and it is bad enough having to face one of them at a time!

23 February

Happy Birthday!

At school this afternoon, we had a lovely birthday party for Luke and Sandra!

Their mothers both brought in some sugared pancakes, and we helped our teacher to set the table in the middle of our dining hall.

The pancakes were delicious! And there were lots of cakes, biscuits and jelly and fruit squash to drink.

Then we had to sing a special song for our two friends. Do you know it?

Happy Birthday to You!
Happy Birthday to You!
Happy Birthday,
Luke and Sandra!
Happy Birthday to You!

We all had a lovely time – especially Luke and Sandra!

24 February

Suddenly, little Elena began to cry!

"Whatever is the matter, dear?" asked our teacher, coming up to her.

"I've got a toothache!" cried poor Elena. "So I can't have any pancakes!"

"Do not worry," grinned a fat boy called Gilbert. "I'll eat your share!"

"There is nothing nice about being greedy, Gilbert!" scolded our teacher.

"Well," said Gilbert, going rather red, "we can roll up Elena's pancake so she can take it home and eat it when her toothache has gone."

"That's a better idea!" smiled teacher. "Well done, Gilbert!"

25 February

Two Clever Creatures!

Billy, the beaver, is the most brilliant builder of the animal world! He lives along our rivers – and although he may not be all that fast on land, he is the most wonderful swimmer, as well as being a fine woodcutter, engineer and bricklayer. His home is called a lodge, which he builds on the river bank, cutting little wooden logs and cementing them together with mud. The beaver also builds a dam on the water in order to protect his home. He even makes two doors, one under the water and one at ground level. Unfortunately, the beaver is a rodent which is nearing extinction in Europe, because, for a long time, it was hunted for meat and for its fur. Nowadays it is protected by law.

26 February

Perhaps the most likeable animal friend is the red squirrel. He lives in cone-bearing trees, building his little nest or "drey" at the very top. The little claws on his feet mean that he can climb tree trunks easily. Squirrels may be timid, but they often come into our parks and our gardens. It is also quite easy to tame them, by feeding them regularly. But the squirrel can be very absent-minded! Although he is good at stocking up food for the winter, he often forgets where he has hidden it!

27 February

A Surprise Visit!

Katy's class at school was going on an outing to a Natural History Museum. It was the first time she had ever been to such a place, so she was very excited. They were going to see the skeleton of a whale, lots of stuffed animals – and it was a lovely coach ride to get there! "This is great!" cried Katy, seeing the big display cases full of birds and animals, silent and still, yet so lifelike. Her friend, Damien, was a bit scared – but he did not like to say anything in front of the others!

"Let's go through here," he whispered to her. "I'm sure there's something that we haven't seen yet. I heard Teacher talking about prehistoric animals...."

28 February

So they went off together. Soon, Katy was so interested in what she saw, that she forgot everything and everybody! "We seem to be the only ones here," she said at last. "What time is it?" "Twelve o'clock!" cried Damien, looking at his watch. "And that's when the museum closes!" "The toilet window!" he went on. "We might be able to get out there!" And luckily for them, the school bus was waiting – outside the toilets! "Even being at school," Damien said afterwards, "is better than being left behind with the dinosaurs!"

29 February

Spring will soon be here!

Winter can often seem to be a sad time, and this is because there are no flowers. And without flowers, there are no colours! Where are the buttercups, the daffodils, the daisies and the cornflowers? It's too cold for any of them to start appearing, yet.

But, beneath the soil, bulbs and roots are growing, little by little, ready to bring forth their flowers.

"I," said the daisy, "I shall wear a lovely, white dress with a big, yellow buttonhole!"

"But it will be a long time before you are ready!" said the snowdrop. "My flowers are appearing, even when it snows. I'm not afraid of the snow!"

Of course, Amanda and Nicholas do not hear the flowers talking. All the same, Amanda is surprised to find that she can pick a bunch of flowers to take home, even though it is winter! Beneath the ground, the daffodil had something to say. "Do not be too proud, snowdrops! Each of us will appear at the right time, even though it may not be just now. You will not see me above the ground until all the ice and snow is well and truly gone!"

"That goes for me, too!" said the poppy. "I have to stay beneath the ground for the whole of the spring!"

High up in the tree, Blackie the blackbird has no idea what the flowers are saying. He just keeps repeating his song for spring-time, practising morning and night, to make sure he is ready for when the colours of the flowers appear again.

1 March

The School Party

We had a Fancy Dress Party at our school today!

Instead of afternoon lessons, we all went into the hall. We were told we could each give four points – one for the most original, one for the most beautiful, one for the most colourful and one for the funniest costume.

Well, the parade began.

Everyone taking part walked around the stage one by one before going back into the wings.

Then they all lined up for us to have one last look before the curtain was lowered.

Half an hour later, the Head Teacher read out the results. We all held our breath, waiting to hear who had won prizes!

2 March

"The most beautiful costume," said Mrs. Bramley, "goes to Martine as a Countess!" We were all pleased about that. "And for the most original costume, Christopher the pedlar! Well done, Christopher!"

"Stephen as Harlequin gets the prize for the most colourful costume," continued Mrs. Bramley, "and for the funniest costume, Julie's clown wins the prize!"

Each winner also got a little medal. Then it was time for the disco, with sweets and streamers for everyone. What a wonderful party it was!

3 March

The Jay and the Woodpecker

Tic-Toc! Tic-Tic-Toc! Can you think what that sound is, coming from the trees in the forest? You might think it is a little hammer – but it is really Willy Woodpecker! With his long, pointed beak, he pecks at the bark of the old trees, hoping to get to the insects underneath. He likes ants, best! And do you know how he catches them? Well, he flicks out his tongue, long and fine, like a thread, into the needles of the fir-tree and traps them there. What's more, this beautiful bird, with his green and yellow feathers and crimson head, builds the most wonderful nest in hollow trees. Suddenly he is disturbed by a sharp, ugly cry just a short distance away.... What can it be?

4 March

It's a jay! He is a bit like a guardian of the forest, warning other birds and animals of any danger.
Not that anyone walking along would see anything!
Then, the jay will fly away, showing off his beautiful feathery coat, striped with blue, white and black. The jay feeds mainly on acorns which he will collect from quite far afield, then forget where he has put them. He will also attack the nests of other birds who are not as strong as he is, eating their eggs and their chicks.

5 March

Snow-White and the Seven Dwarfs

There was once a king, who, after his first wife died, married a woman who was as evil as she was beautiful. This king had a lovely daughter called Snow-White – and the new queen, who was also a witch, hated her from the very beginning.

Now the wicked queen had a magic mirror, and one day the mirror said that Snow-White was the fairest in the land. The queen was furious and decided to put her to death. But Snow-White, helped by one of the queen's guards, escaped into the forest. There she came across a little cottage where the seven dwarfs lived, and they said Snow-White could stay with them. She did the housework and looked after them all, and they loved her in return.

6 March

Meanwhile, thanks to her magic mirror, the wicked queen had discovered where Snow-White was. She turned herself into an old woman, and poisoned the rosiest-looking apple she could find. Then off she went into the forest, planning to give the poisoned apple to Snow-White. And the moment Snow-White took a bite, she fell to the ground in a dead faint. The seven dwarfs believed she was dead, and laid her in a crystal casket which they set down in her favourite part of the forest.

7 March

One day, a handsome prince happened to be riding through the forest. And the moment he saw Snow-White, he felt he just had to lift the lid of the crystal casket and give her a kiss. At once, Snow-White opened her eyes and smiled at him. The evil spell which the wicked queen had cast upon her was broken!

How the seven dwarfs rejoiced! And soon after, they rejoiced again when Snow-White and the handsome young prince were married.

8 March

The Talking Parrot

Mrs. Duncombe had bought a red and green parrot. Every day she taught him some new words and Coco could repeat them easily.

Perhaps, a little too easily....

One day, Mrs. Duncombe invited her three friends to tea, so that they could see her wonderful parrot.

It was something which she soon wished she had not done.

Coco was such a chatterbox that none of the ladies could get a word in edgeways!

9 March

Which Way Does the Wind Blow?

Pippa woke up during the night, trembling with fear. Outside, the wind sounded so fierce and so strong, and it seemed to shake the whole house. And what was that story she had heard – about the three little pigs and the wolf blowing their house in? Even the thought of it made her start trembling all over again!

"Daddy!" she cried at the top of her voice. "Mummy! I'm frightened!" Daddy reached her bedside first. He comforted his little daughter, hugging her close against him.

"What's the matter?" he asked her.

"It – it's that noise!" sobbed Pippa. "Where is it coming from?"

10 March

"That's only the wind!" Daddy told her gently. "Nothing to be frightened of!"

"Do you know something?" he went on. "The wind can be useful. Once, I remember walking near the sea with my grandfather. He showed me how to tell the direction of the wind, by showing me a weather-vane on top of an old church tower. Just a few hours later, I found I was lost in a strange town. Without grandfather telling me about the wind, then seeing the weather-vane on the church tower, I would never have been able to find my way back to where we were staying."

11 March

The Court Jesters Are Here!

All the pavements in the little town were thick with people. "Just wait, son!" said Graham's Dad. "The parade of the Court Jesters is something to see!"
Graham held on to his Mum and Dad's hands, trying to see through the crowds, jostling around and enjoying themselves. Then suddenly, he heard music – brass, drums and bells!
His Dad lifted him up on to his shoulders so that he could see everything. And as he watched the parade, Graham's eyes opened wide. What a sight it was! And what a clatter from the clogs which the jesters wore, as they marched along! But, what were they wearing on their heads?

12 March

All their hats were decorated with white and coloured feathers, swaying to the rhythm of the music. Then, hundreds of oranges were thrown in all directions, smashing against the walls and the shutters over the windows. Graham clapped hard, wishing he could show his friends one of the oranges thrown by the famous jesters. At that moment, a jester stopped, giving Graham a special smile. Graham held his breath, then – hurrah! He caught the orange which the jester threw! It was a day he would never forget!

13 March

Jeremy is Ill

It's raining outside, the wind is blowing a gale and Jeremy is away from school because he has 'flu. And how long the days seem without his friends! No wonder he is feeling bored, all by himself. Daddy has gone to work, Mummy is busy with the housework. There's only Bobo, the dog, at the side of Jeremy's bed. Bobo knows his young master is sick, so he is content just to watch him and lick his hand every so often.

"Nobody has come to see me," says Jeremy sadly. "Not even for a little while...."

"Now, don't fret," says his mother, bathing his forehead with a sponge. "The doctor said you were to stay in bed and rest." Just then, the door bell rings. Who could it be?

14 March

Jeremy has a visitor after all! It is Mr. Lewis, his teacher. "And how is the patient, today?" he smiles.

"Sir," groans Jeremy, "I'm so bored!"

"You'll soon be on your feet," says his teacher. "Look, your friends at school have asked me to bring you this letter. They've all signed it!"

Jeremy opens the envelope and reads the letter. "We all hope that you will soon get better," it ends. "We miss you a lot."

Jeremy's eyes begin to shine, just a little. Do you think this is because he has the 'flu?

15 March

The Mini Fair

Fishing for ducks... a shooting gallery... sideshows.... Is it really necessary to go to a fair to enjoy all these? Of course, not! Here are a few ideas to help your imagination along! For fishing rods, try using off-cuts of wood, bamboo, cane or garden sticks, with a length of string and a little magnet tied at one end.

And, the ducks? They can always be disguised as empty drinks cans hidden behind the back of a chair! (If the can sticks to the inside rim of your refrigerator door, then you can use it for your game!) Remember to leave the pull-ring in place, too.

Use our picture as a guide for setting up the game – and sort out whatever you like for prizes!

16 March

Do you like games where you have to throw things? Nearly everyone does! So why not try making a shooting gallery?

First, mark out a face on a large cardboard box – something like a clown, where a large hole can be cut for the mouth. Then you can put an empty bottle at either side and try to throw a quoit or plastic bangle over the neck. It's a good excuse for inviting friends in to play. After all, it isn't every day that you can enjoy all the fun of the fair in your own home!

17 March

The First Signs of Spring

The trees may still be bare, but we always know that spring is around the corner, when we see little green shoots appearing.

The hazel tree will soon have golden catkins, hanging down like sugar candy! Blow gently underneath, and the tree will send down a little cloud of golden pollen.

And what a lovely carpet of flowers begins to appear on the ground, making the most of the rays of the sun which shine down through the bare branches of the trees!

It is easy to see the buttercup, because of its pretty bright yellow flower. Then there is the primrose, queen of the spring-time flowers, and, in a little glade, a whole cluster of violets.

18 March

Click-clack-click! Here comes a spell of bad weather, with little white balls clattering down on the roofs of houses and rolling on the ground! It is one of those showers which often happen without warning in March. Cold winds bring the showers on, but, luckily, they do not last more than a few minutes – just long enough to cover everything with a fine, pearly carpet which melts in the first rays of sunshine. The sky clears quickly, and, best of all, when we see these sudden showers of hailstones, we know that winter is well and truly over.

19 March

A Surprise on the Pond.....

What has been happening on the pond? The ice has melted and there is life everywhere. Croak-croak! Mr. and Mrs. Frog are happy enough, diving in and out of the water. "I've laid thousands of eggs!" Mrs. Frog croaks proudly to her husband. And, sure enough, clusters of frog spawn float on the water.

From the centre of each egg will come a tadpole, the frog's young.

"In a few days," says Mrs. Frog, "each tadpole will leave its egg and swim just like a fish!"

"But we can also jump around on the ground," added her husband.

"Yes," agreed his wife, "but the tadpoles have to learn to live in the water first! Then, do you know what happens?"

20 March

"Of course!" croaks Mr. Frog. "Little by little, our young ones will lose their tails, which they use as a fin, and become more like us!"

"Not so fast!" says Mrs. Frog. "Have you forgotten two pairs of feet with long claws to replace the fin for getting around?"

"Oh, yes! Then they can leave the water and become amphibians like us, able to live on land as well as in water!"

"So we must keep watch," says Mrs. Frog. "And see that the ducks do not come and eat up our eggs!"

The Spring

Spring-time is here!
Winter is over at last!
The air feels softer, the sun warms our faces...
Everywhere looks so different, with the land changing its white blanket for a new, colourful cloak, dazzling with new life.
The birds end the long silence, singing their songs to welcome the spring.
There is plenty of food to feed their growing families, now! Flowers appear in the twinkling of an eye.
Buds open out on the trees, which spread out their new branches.
As for Mr. Hedgehog, he gives a big yawn, and sniffs the spring-time air!
"What time is it?" he wonders. "I think I have slept long enough!"

21 March

22 March

Jack and the Beanstalk

There was once a poor boy called Jack, who lived in the country with his mother.
One day, Jack's mother asked him to go to market to sell their cow. On the way, Jack met a man who said he would give him three magic beans for the animal.
Jack's mother was furious!
Fancy handing over their only cow for three beans!
All the same, Jack believed that the beans really were magic.
He planted them right in front of their house.
Very quickly, they grew into an enormous beanstalk, reaching right up to the sky!
Jack soon decided he had to climb to the top and see what was up there!

23 March

He found himself climbing right up into the clouds – and there, he discovered a great, big castle! Jack went towards the nearest door, opened it and went inside. This door led into the dining room, where the giant who owned the castle – so huge that he was frightening to see – was having a meal. And when he had finished eating, Jack saw him go over to a little white hen which was on a cushion nearby and pick up a golden egg she had just laid!
Then the giant went to sleep in an armchair. This was Jack's chance to pick up the little hen.....

24 March

With the hen under his arm, Jack ran towards the top of the magic beanstalk. But the giant had heard his footsteps, and came running after him!
As fast as he could, Jack clambered down the beanstalk, then ran to get the biggest axe he could find!
One blow of that axe, and the beanstalk came crashing down, with the giant falling down with it.
And from then on, the little white hen laid a golden egg for Jack every day. He and his mother would never want for anything, ever again.

25 March

Indoor Games

"We get bored, being indoors all the time!"

How many times have you heard that? So, what about the Green-Pea Game? Or Pinning the Tail on the Donkey? Perhaps you have forgotten these – or maybe you do not know them?

Well, for the Green-Pea Game, you need just six dried or frozen peas, two saucers and a straw. Then all you have to do is to see how quickly you can get the peas from one saucer to another by sucking them up at the end of the straw. Touch one of the peas with your hands, and you are out of the game! It can be a race as well as a game of skill. But with a little bit of practice, you can soon become quite an expert!

26 March

Pinning the Tail on the Donkey needs a little more preparation. First of all, draw a donkey on a piece of cardboard or paper, then cut this out, ready to pin on a wall. A few strands of wool tied together at one end will be the donkey's tail – and each player has to try putting it in the right place with the aid of a drawing pin....

The difficult part is that each player also has to wear a blindfold!

Just wait and see what funny places the donkey is supposed to swish its tail!

27 March

A Strange Kind of Medicine.....

Today is quite special, because this evening, there is to be a disco party at school! Unfortunately, Laurence does not feel too well when he wakes up. His head feels hot, and his feet feel cold. His cheeks are flushed bright red, and he is sneezing. "Oh, no!" he says aloud. "I cannot be ill!"

"But," he adds, with another sneeze, "I cannot go to school like this! But what can I do to get better? Mummy mustn't know, that's for sure...."

Then Laurence remembers seeing some Red Indian Medicine Men on television, making up the most wonderful potions to cure sick people really quickly.

"I'll try doing that," he thinks.

28 March

Without making a sound, Laurence goes downstairs and into the kitchen. He opens the cupboard, taking out every single thing he thinks will do him good – honey, cinnamon, golden syrup, jam, cocoa, and lots of other things! Then he stirs this strange mixture in a big bowl, gulping it all down in one swallow.

Almost straight away, he has a terrible tummy-ache!

"Ow-ow!" moans Laurence. "There must be something else which the Medicine Men did! Quick! Call Mummy! And the doctor!"

29 March

Let's Play Hopscotch!

Mrs. Dawkins decided to make the most of the fine weather by washing the tiles along her garden path. And she was very proud of her work! "That's a good job done!" she said, smiling. "Now, to get on with the washing...."

Not long afterwards, Nadine, Lee, Theresa and Alan came along. They were on holiday from school and wondering what to do on such a beautiful day.

"Shall we play Hopscotch?" Theresa suggested. "Look, I've got some chalk!"

"And I've got four counters," added Lee, feeling in his pockets.

The two boys began chalking lines on Mrs. Dawkins' clean garden path! What on earth would she say?

30 March

Next, the two boys shared out the counters.

"Who's first?" asked Nadine.

Just then, Mrs. Dawkins came out of her house. The children knew something must be wrong, from the way she looked at the chalk marks.

"Well, that does not seem too serious!" said the old lady at last. "You can carry on playing!"

"Thank you, Mrs. Dawkins!" said the children. "We'll wash your path afterwards!"

"That," smiled Mrs. Dawkins, "is a good idea, a very good idea, indeed!"

31 March

The Fox and the Raven

A big, black raven was feeling very proud of himself. For many days, he had been watching the dairyman who sold cheeses – dozens of cheeses of all shapes and sizes!

Now, as soon as the man's back was turned, the raven picked out the one he wanted. Then he flew high up in a tree, carrying the cheese in his beak. What a fine feast he would have, the raven thought to himself!

Down on the ground, the fox came towards the tree without a sound. He had already smelt the cheese, and, as he'd had nothing to eat for three days, he was feeling very hungry indeed.

The fox was also very crafty.

"Good day, Raven!" he said politely. "My, what a handsome bird you are! Such lovely feathers! You say hardly a word, and yet your voice must surely be so deep and beautiful!"

The raven listened, keeping the cheese firmly in his beak. But, he thought, if the fox wanted to hear him speak, he could not disappoint him.... So, the raven opened his beak – and, out fell the cheese!

The fox snapped it up at once and ran away to eat it in peace!

Which just goes to show that the flatterer always wins at the expense of the one who listens!

1 April

April Fool!

The first day of April is the day when we play jokes on people.

Paul always looks forward to it. The trouble is, he can never think of anything very funny to do.

Last year, for instance, he tried painting the goldfish blue – until his Dad came in and stopped him. Julie and Mandy, his sisters, remember only too well some of the cruel tricks he has played on them in the past! So, today, they have decided to play a trick on Paul and get their own back!

Now, everyone knows that Paul can be very greedy – he likes eating cakes best of all.

Little does he know that he is in for quite a surprise.....

2 April

For more than an hour, Julie and Mandy have been in the kitchen, putting the finishing touches to their surprise cake. Paul is getting very impatient.

"Haven't you finished, yet?" he keeps asking.

"Here it is!" they call out at last. And they put a huge cake down on the table in front of him. It looks so delicious that Paul cannot wait to taste it! He grabs a knife, ready to cut himself a big slice – only to find that the blade does not even make a mark. Julie and Mandy have made the cake with modelling clay!

3 April

Bella Goes to Rome

"All roads lead to Rome..." – so the saying goes. But for Bella, the little bell, things were not quite so simple.... She had left her village the evening before, and now, she was well on her way.

"Excuse me, Swallow," she said, "but can you tell me how to get to Rome?"

"Fly to the east!" advised the swallow. "Fly over the Alps and you will arrive in Italy. Then go right until you get to Rome!"

"Thank you!" cried Bella. And on she flew, going exactly the way the swallow had told her.

"There's a mountain ahead," Bella thought. "My goodness, it's high! Good thing I'm not afraid of heights. But it gets colder, the higher I go, and there's still some snow here..."

4 April

It took some time for Bella to fly over the snow-covered peaks.

"Atishoo!" she sneezed. "Oh, dear! I've caught a cold!"

And passing through a valley, Bella grabbed an old scarf which had caught on a hedge. She did not want to have a bad chest!

At last, the little bell came to Rome, ready to get her store of chocolate eggs for Easter.

"You are the last customer!" the shopkeeper told her. "Take these back with you and hurry along! Do not get lost on the way!"

5 April

The Hen Which Laid the Golden Eggs

There was once a farmer who was always complaining because his hens could never each lay an egg every day. He tried changing their feed for special grains which were supposed to help them lay more eggs – but it was no good.

The poor hens did all they could, but the farmer was never satisfied. Then, one day, as the farmer felt among the straw, he saw something shining – it was a beautiful golden egg!

He had a hen who laid golden eggs! He took the hen in his arms, wondering for a moment if he were dreaming. But, no – it really was true. The little hen was quite real.

6 April

The farmer set the hen aside from the others and put her in a place which was quiet and cosy, trying to make her comfortable.

He was always feeding her, doing all he could to see that she would lay lots of golden eggs each day.

Then he kept lifting her up, feeling around in the straw, hoping to find more and more golden eggs each time he looked.

The little hen was very patient.

But the day came when she felt that she had suffered enough.

7 April

Instead of golden eggs, she decided, she would lay one ordinary egg each day, like the other hens.

When the farmer flew into a rage, the little hen said she would not lay eggs at all! The other hens said they would do the same, unless they got more kindness. It seemed that the farm would come to a standstill.

The farmer knew then that he would have to treat his hens much better, learning the lesson that nobody should take advantage of those who work hard.

They might just be stronger than anyone imagines....

8 April

It's a Dog's Life!

Yola is a little black and white dog, and she is very well cared for by her owners. The only thing is, that the family have to leave her alone all day because they are either at school or at work. When the weather is fine, Yola likes to sit outside her kennel in the sun. But, this morning, it is raining, and nobody is in! If only she had not barked to be let out into the garden! Now, she is sulking a little. When will they come back, she wonders?

9 April

Giving Out the Eggs

What a journey! Bella the little bell is worn out, but at least she has returned safely! She has had to go through a snow-storm over the mountains, only just managing to keep hold of her precious little bundles! Now, at last, she is back home in the little village where she lives.

During the night, she drops the chocolate eggs into the gardens, before going back to the church bell tower. She sleeps like a log, and when morning comes, the priest pulls the bell rope so that she sings again, waking everyone up with her merry sound.

All the children, many with breakfast toast still in their hands, jump up and come running out.

What will they find?

10 April

From all parts of the village comes the cry, "Thank you, Bella! Thank you for the eggs!"

And Bella, seeing the happy faces of all the children, forgets how tired she is and all the dangers of her long journey to Rome – the mountains, the snow, the strong winds… It all seems worthwhile, just to see the joy in the eyes of all the villagers. So, when you pass by the church, do not forget to smile up at the bell right at the top of the tower, will you? It is sure to make Bella very, very happy!

11 April

Lots of Nests!

Cheep-cheep-cheep! What's that noise coming from the undergrowth? What is happening?

A pretty Blue Tit hops around on the grass looking for worms. And in the middle of a little bush, away from prying eyes and sheltered by the pine trees, there is a round, cosy-looking nest made out of twigs and feathers. When she hears anyone coming, the mother tit covers up her four pink, speckled eggs.

So, if you know of any birds' nests, be sure not to disturb them. More important still, do not take any of the eggs!

In a few days, you may be lucky enough to see some baby chicks, their little beaks wide open, ready for their parents to feed them.

12 April

Birds' nests are curious things. They can come in all shapes and sizes – round and flat, above the ground, on the ground....

A moorhen even builds a floating nest. As for the green woodpecker, he builds his nest in tree trunks.

Swallows build their nests under the eaves of roofs and gutter-pipes, and sometimes inside farm buildings.

In spring, all birds build or plan their nests. Many return to the same place year after year to nest, often using the same one for their young each year!

13 April

Mr. Giles and His Garden

Old Mr. Giles had broken his ankle, so he was feeling rather miserable – especially when he could not do anything in his kitchen garden.
Tina, Rosalie and Sam were talking about it.
"I'd like to do something for nice, old Mr. Giles," began Tina.
"He's such a kind, old man," added Sam. "Do you remember how he mended my bike?"
"Well, we are on holiday," Rosalie reminded them. "So why don't we help by tidying his garden?"
"It would be a nice surprise!" agreed Sam.
"Good idea!" said the others, big smiles on their faces.
So, what do you think they did?

14 April

The children set to work at once. And two hours later, it was all finished.
Then, looking rather dirty, they went to the front door and rang the bell.
Mr. Giles gave a groan and heaved himself out of his armchair, reaching for his crutches so that he could go and see who it was.
"We have a surprise for you!" cried the children. "Come and see!"
Looking rather puzzled, Mr. Giles followed them outside… And when he saw his garden, he was lost for words! But how pleased and proud the three friends were!

15 April

All Nature Celebrates!

During the month of April, the whole of nature is so beautiful with its colours and the lovely scents of the flowers. So it is a good time to take a leaf out of nature's book and make the most of spring!

Look around and you are sure to get lots of ideas for toys and decorations, using nature's gifts... a skirt of ferns or weeping willow, daisy chains, a bracelet of buttercups... or how about making a wig from dried grass?

Boys might like to try making a bow and arrow from a hazel branch and a piece of string. Or perhaps a spear made from a piece of wood, tapered at one end.

There are lots of ways we can use just about everything that we see!

16 April

Just as the sun brings out the colours of the flowers, we can also brighten up our faces.

There are many ways of doing this, without using paints or powders – and you do not have to think about borrowing any of Mum's make-up, either!

Of course, you can buy packs of stage grease-paint... but there are lots of other things you can use. A little beaten egg-white is the perfect base for sticking petals, leaves and flowers on your face for a spring-time mask!

Mimi and the Cuckoo

"That bird is getting on my nerves!" thought Mimi, the kitten. "The next time he dares to put the tip of his beak outside..... I-I'll get him!"
But Mimi did not know one important fact. The cuckoo she hated so much was made of wood, and only came out of the clock to tell the time!
Well, the minutes passed, and Mimi waited. Then – tick-tick-tock! Suddenly, the little door in the clock opened and the bird appeared.
"Cuckoo! Cuckoo!" Mimi leapt up and reached out her paw. But instead of hitting the bird, she caught the pendulum, which broke and fell to the floor. So, instead of getting the bird, she got a good hiding instead!

17 April

18 April

The Donkey Coat

There was once a king who was very sad, because his wife, whom he had loved very much, had died.
Now, this king had a daughter who was very much like his poor wife. And one day, he decided that she should marry.
But, as the princess kept telling her father, she did not want to get married!
At last, she went to see her Fairy Godmother, who told the princess to ask her father for the most wonderful gown, the colour of moonlight. This the princess did. And a few days later, the king brought her a splendid gown made of feather-light material, embroidered with silver thread and with a cape like a cloud to wear over it.

19 April

Having granted his daughter's wish, the king again began to talk about her getting married. So, following the advice of her Fairy Godmother once again, the princess then asked for a gown the colour of sunlight.

The king granted her wish at once. And what a magical gown it was! Woven from golden thread, it gleamed and shone like the brightest star. The slightest movement made it sparkle like a thousand little lights. There were hundreds of golden beads sewn all over it and a girdle of gold to match.

Then, the princess asked the king for the skin of a donkey.... and once again, her father was only too pleased to grant her wish.

And still the king wanted his daughter to get married. So, what could she do?

20 April

The princess put on the donkey skin and left the palace, finding work as a maid at an inn. One day, a young prince came by and saw "Donkey Coat", as the princess was known. That evening, seeing her without the skin, he thought how beautiful she was. After that he called every day, and when he asked her to marry him, she agreed at once.

The prince went to the palace. The king was so happy to see his daughter, that he began planning the most wonderful wedding celebrations!

21 April

A Box – and a Surprise!

Every day, Ella went outside to open the post-box. But one particular morning, she got quite a surprise! Underneath the envelopes, she could feel something rather strange....

"Oh!" she cried. "Where have these five little eggs come from? There must be a family of blue tits, and they think they've found the perfect place to build their nest!"

"It's very nice...." she thought to herself, "but what shall I do? If I leave the eggs here, they could be crushed by something in the post. But I know I should not disturb them..."

Ella gave a big sigh. She just did not have the heart to move them out. So, she thought for a few more minutes. And then, she had an idea!

22 April

In the shed, Ella found an old wooden box.

"It won't take long to make another post-box," she thought, "something we can use until the chicks are born..."

Very sensibly, Ella took the trouble to tie up the door of the first post-box, leaving the hole clear, so that the birds could fly in and out.

Then, she wrote a note to pin at the bottom.

DO NOT DISTURB, MR. POSTMAN!
THIS IS THE BLUE-TITS' HOUSE!

23 April

One Swallow does not make a Summer!

The swallows have come back, so now, everyone knows that spring really is here! Everyone loves to see them with their glossy blue backs and lovely white throats.

And as well as being lovely birds, they are also very brave and strong. Did you know that they fly all the way back from Africa, crossing the widest oceans? Every year they return to nest in the same places, building nests of dried mud.

But do not muddle the swallow with the swift! You can recognise the swift by the big circles which it makes as it flies in the sky. When it flies high, a fine day is supposed to be in store. And when it flies low, then rain is surely on its way!

24 April

Cuckoo! Cuckoo! Cuckoo! Yes, it's the cuckoo, the bird who lives in woodland. And when the cuckoo sings, it's the start of fine weather! But the cuckoo is very lazy! Instead of building a nest, he uses those of other birds! No wonder they all keep a close guard on their home when they know the cuckoo is around..

Also, the cuckoo never hatches its eggs. Instead, it leaves them for other birds to hatch and to raise the chicks as their own.

Perhaps that is why the cuckoo has so much time to sing!

25 April

Gardening

"Just the day for doing a bit of gardening!" announced Edward's Dad. "The soil is nice and firm, and that's just right to do some digging!" So, Edward got the tools out – a spade to dig the soil and a hoe and a rake to make the ground level.

"Which vegetables do you like, Edward?" asked his Dad, once all the hard work was done.

"I like peas and carrots!" said Edward. "They're my favourites!"

"Right!" smiled Dad. "But I think we'll also need to plant some potatoes and lettuces, as well! We'd better go along to the garden centre, don't you think?" And soon, Edward and his father were planting lots of vegetables. Do you know what they had to do?

26 April

First, they made long, straight lines in the soil for sewing the seeds and planting out the seed potatoes. And as they worked, Edward's father explained all about the different vegetables.

"Potatoes and those carrots which you like so much, they are root vegetables, so they grow beneath the soil. Lettuces, cabbages and peas all these grow above the soil."

After that, Edward had only one question on his mind.

"When shall we be able to make vegetable soup?"

27 April

Make a Collage!

Here is something which you can do on those April days when showers are in the air!

All you need is some paper, gum or paste, scissors and some old leaflets, magazines, brochures....

Just make sure before you begin that nobody wants them!

Find a sheet of plain paper. Then you are ready to begin making a collage picture. Cut out sections of pictures and put them together to make something quite different....

Perhaps you could paste a cow sitting up in a palm tree, or stick a camel on top of a mountain!

You could give a horse the head of a lion, or the lion, the face of a boy.... perhaps, somebody you know?

28 April

There are many ways of framing a collage, and lots of things you can use for this, too.

You could think about making a border of seeds, tissue paper, rice, lace, buttons – or even broken spaghetti pieces!

And if you want to make sure that your collage lasts a long time, it is worth taking the trouble to stick it on to a firm backing of cardboard, so cut from a box or supermarket carton. Just remember that the heavier your collage is, the thicker your backing will need to be.

The Hare and the Tortoise

There was once a young hare who lived in the heart of the country. He was a very handsome hare, and so fast on his feet, that he was quite sure nobody could ever beat him. He liked to make fun of the other animals, especially a little tortoise. "You're so clumsy-looking!" he would say. "Why, just look at your short, little legs and your stubby, little head! And how slow you always are!" One day, the tortoise decided that he'd had enough of the hare's unkind remarks. "You think you can run fast on your long legs and big feet! But mine, short as they are, can go just as fast!"

29 April

30 April

"Don't you believe me?" went on the tortoise. "Then I'll give you a race!" "All right!" laughed the hare. At a signal from the fox, the two started off. The tortoise lost no time in going along as fast as he could. But the hare, full of scorn for the tortoise, thought he might as well have a nice nap on the grass... After all, he thought, he would have plenty of time to catch up and win the race! But when he woke – why, the tortoise was at the finishing line! He had won the race and beaten that boastful hare!

1 May

A May-Day Holiday!

"The 1st of May is a holiday!
Put down your work,
And have some play!"
Three friends laughed as they finished their May Day song. Then Diana said, "It's the day for picking Lily-of-the-Valley! Do you know where we can find some?"
"Where?" asked Simon.
"On that patch of ground by the church, hidden behind a few big stones. Come on, let's pick some."
"Good idea!" cried Eric.

They soon reached the place that Diana had told them about. Then all three began picking the Lily-of-the-Valley flowers from the hundreds which were there, enjoying the feel of the pearly-white blossom and the long, glossy, green leaves.
Before long, they had picked all they needed. They took it home and gave it to all their friends and neighbours. Some people gave them money in return, so they went to the sweet-shop to buy something nice.
"My mother says that sweets ruin our teeth!" groaned Eric.
"Mine, too!" sighed Diana. Then she brightened up. "Suppose we spend the money going swimming instead?"
And, as they agreed afterwards, that was the perfect way of spending a May Day holiday!

The Four-Leaf Clover

Ever since Felix had heard somebody saying that a four-leaf clover was supposed to be lucky, he had searched non-stop for one in every field and meadow.

"What are you doing, Felix?" asked the old brown cow.

"Picking four-leaf clovers!" he said. "They're very lucky, you know!"

"They've never brought me much luck," mooed the cow, "and I've often eaten them! Instead of wasting time with your nose on the ground, you'd do better helping your mother with her work on the farm. Just think how lucky she will feel then, having a son like you."

It sounded so nice that Felix decided to take the cow's advice. And he was not sorry that he did.

2 May

3 May

The Three Little Pigs

There were once three little pigs who each wanted a house of his own.

The first built his house of straw. It did not seem very strong, but at least it was finished quickly. The first little pig did not like hard work!

The second pig built his house of wood. This was stronger, but the second pig disliked work as much as the first. He was therefore content to stick the planks together, instead of using nails and doing the job properly. And the third little pig? It took him a long time to build a house of bricks, but it was solid and the windows and doors closed firmly. It was a very strong little house.

4 May

But the third little pig was often teased by his brothers.
"Don't you ever want to play?" they asked him. "Be like us and have some fun once in a while! Playing around is much nicer than working!"
Then came the day when a big wolf arrived, hunting for food! The three pigs each took shelter in their homes. First, the wolf went up to the house of straw. Just a few huffs and puffs from him, and it tumbled to the ground! And when the first little pig ran off to the house built of wood, the wolf chased after him!

5 May

Inside, the two little pigs trembled with fear. And when the wolf blew down the house of wood, too, they only just managed to escape to the brick-built house! Now, the wolf was very angry... He tried huffing and puffing harder than ever, but it was no good! The house had been so well-built that it stood firm, and in the end, the wolf went away, tired out. The first two little pigs had to admit that they had been wrong to mock their brother and each began to build a good, strong house. As for that wicked wolf – he never came back.

6 May

From Caterpillar to Butterfly.....

A butterfly can often be as colourful as the brightest summer flower. Yet only a few months before, it was a funny-looking, furry caterpillar.

To avoid the frosts, it became a chrysalis, spending the whole of the winter sheltered in the branch of a tree. Now, the fine weather has returned, and the magnificent butterfly can spread its wings and leave its winter home. The one in the picture is taking nectar from the flowers.

Soon, Mother Butterfly will lay her eggs in the folds of nettle leaves. Then, her eggs will become caterpillars, then chrysales, and, at last, butterflies once more.

7 May

Would you like to go on a butterfly hunt? All you need is a net on a stick, a jam jar and a lid or a piece of paper to cover it with a few holes in it.

Then, go gently towards the flower where you see a butterfly. It may be difficult because butterflies are very shy, and they soon fly away. But you should be able to net one long enough to get a good look at its beautiful wings, before letting it go again.

More than anything else, butterflies need their space and their freedom in order to live.

8 May

Happy Birthday, Mummy!

It's Mummy's birthday today!
Daddy, Jessica and Stephen have each bought her a present and they all give her a special hug, too.
Only Gillian has nothing to give, because she has spent all her pocket money! Now she wishes she hadn't.
Without a word, the little girl goes out of the house, wondering what she can do to make up for it.
She finds herself wandering down to the fields where the cows are grazing quietly and the farmer and his dog are leading the sheep to pasture.
Suddenly, Gillian has an idea!
She begins picking a lovely bunch of wild flowers, feeling a lot happier.
Then, she runs all the way home, and goes straight to her bedroom, closing the door firmly behind her.

A few minutes later, Gillian finds her mother in the kitchen.
She does not say anything at first. But her Mummy sees that her eyes are lowered and her hands are behind her back. Gillian's heart is also beating fast.
"Mummy," she says at last, "I'm sorry that I spent all my pocket money and forgot your birthday...."
She goes up to her mother and holds out the bunch of flowers.
"Happy Birthday, Mummy!" she says, as nicely as she can. "I love you lots!"
"More than sweets and chocolate and all the other things you buy with your pocket money?" smiles Mummy.
"Of course I do!" Gillian smiles back at her.
"Then," says Mummy, "I forgive you, my little feather-brain!"

9 May

Pippin, the Little Bird

Pippin was a little bird who lived in the country. "How dull your life must be, Pippin," said a seagull one day, "just flying from tree to tree without ever seeing anything else! I travel everywhere, from the sea to the wide, open spaces!"

"That's true!" Pippin sighed. "I do not care what anyone says! I must fly away from here, right away! I can't stand this dull life a moment longer!"

Pippin felt so proud as he flew towards the stream, then the river flowing down to the sea.

"Wonderful!" he cried, quite forgetting how tired he felt after such a long journey.

10 May

When Pippin first reached the sea, it all looked much more beautiful than the country. But when he searched for somewhere to rest and something to eat, things were different. On the advice of another seagull, he perched on the mast of a ship.

"This is terrible!" he thought. "The trees back home did not move like this!" Then, he had his first taste of fish.

"Ugh!" he cried in disgust. "I could never eat that!"

Perhaps, he thought, living in the country was not so bad, after all....

11 May

Luke and the Swing-Ball

When Luke's grandparents returned from holiday, they brought him back the very latest Swing-Ball!
Luke was very pleased.
He decided to go and show it to his friends, so he went to the park where they all met.
"Look, Alan!" he cried proudly. "My Grandma and Grandpa bought me this Swing-Ball!"
"Great!" yelled Alan.
"Let's have a game!" grinned Mark.
"Oh, no!" said Luke. "It's my Swing-Ball! You lot are only allowed to watch!"
And he put a block of wood on the ground and began unrolling the elastic.
Then, he began hitting the ball with his bat.

12 May

The others soon got tired of watching.
One by one, they left the play-park, until Luke was quite alone.
He began feeling sorry for himself, and sorry for the way he had behaved.
"Come on!" he said to his friends, "let's have a proper match, shall we? This is a terrific game for four players!"
"All right!" said Tom.
"Let's choose sides!" said Mark.
"How do we score points?" Alan wanted to know.
Luke could not help being surprised at the number of friends he had!

13 May

Popcorn Magic!

May is the time when all nature seems to be bursting with surprises – like popcorn which you can make with a little help from a grown-up.

You need cooking oil, popping corn from the grocer's, health food shop or supermarket, and sugar. Gently heat two tablespoons of oil in a pan, then add two or three level tablespoons of corn. As if by magic, you will see the grains of corn beginning to swell, before bursting – and popping! To stop them flying all over the kitchen, put a cover over the pan when the corn starts to swell. When all the corn has popped, tip it into a dish and sprinkle with sugar. You will see that home-made popcorn is not only nice to eat, it is also nice to look at.

14 May

Find a drinking straw then stick on a few pieces of popcorn to cover half the length. You can then cut leaves from green paper and stick these at the bottom of the straw.

Do you think it looks like the pretty Lily-of-the-Valley flower?

Or, you can add a few drops of red food colouring to the popcorn to make the pink flowers of hawthorn blossom. Then put your flowers in a freezer dish, half filled with soil, and you have the perfect indoor garden!

15 May

o Bring Good Luck.....

When April goes, the last of the cold weather usually goes with it, leaving us to enjoy the warm weather and blue skies of May. Now, we see lots of Lily-of-the-Valley flowers in our gardens and parks, or growing wild in woodland. Many people believe that these lovely little flowers with their pretty white bells bring good luck to those who give and receive them.
It was once the custom for children to pick bunches of Lily-of-the-Valley to give to their mothers and friends. During May, you can see lots of wild flowers in the towns as well as the country. Some are protected – which means you are not supposed to pick them – but there will usually be a notice about this. Also, if you pick your flowers at the bottom of the stem, take care not to damage the root. Placed in a jar of water, they give a lovely splash of colour in your home!
Or, what about growing a primrose? Try using a spoon to lift one from the soil, so that you take the root as well. Then plant it in a pot half filled with earth, and place on your balcony or window sill. Water it regularly, and it will flower well into the summer months.

16 May

The Joys of Fishing!

So much seems to be happening beside the pond!
Lots of creatures gather here, with lots of chirping and squawking everywhere.
Hares and rabbits have come for a little wash, whilst the deer drink the clear water. Frogs jump from one water-lily to the next, and fish leap up on the surface of the water, quietly catching some flies and midges.
Only the heron is still – because he is such a good fisherman! With his long beak pressed close between his wings, he can keep quite still for an hour or more, waiting for a little fish to come up, then – gulp! In one swallow, the bird has eaten its prey.

17 May

"Let's go fishing!" said Daniel's Grandpa.
"Great!" cried Daniel. "Maybe we'll catch some trout for tea!"
"Not so fast!" Grandpa laughed. "A good fisherman must have patience!"
They set off and very soon Grandpa was ready to begin. He tied a hook very firmly at the end of the line, then threw this into the water with all his might. He was lucky. In just a few minutes, Grandpa was pulling a fine trout out of the water! What a surprise to find that Grandpa did not need to be patient that afternoon!

18 May

The Rainbow

Only five minutes ago, it was fine and sunny. Now it is raining! But the sun has not gone away. It is playing Hide-and-Seek between the clouds. Suddenly – there it is again..... And what beautiful colours appear in the sky... A rainbow!

As the rain falls, the light of the sun is reflected in the raindrops suspended in the sky, making an arch of seven different colours. Learn the colours in their right order, and you could draw a rainbow! They are – red, orange, yellow, green, blue, indigo and violet. All these colours together are called the spectrum. And when they separate, there is nothing.

What about another way to see a rainbow – this time, in your own home?

19 May

Take a small mirror and dip it in a glass of water.

Then move it until the light from the sun falls exactly on to the mirror.

Put a sheet of paper under the reflected light, and you will see the seven colours of the rainbow.

Or try adding a few drops of oil to a basin of soapy water ready for bubble-blowing!

Some bubbles will be big, some small – but you will see the rainbow colours in every one, until they burst into nothing.

20 May

The Water-Lilies

Do you know which flowers Joanne wanted to pick for her Aunt? Water-Lilies! Isn't that a funny idea?
But, Joanne had always loved these strange flowers which seemed to float so gently on the surface of the pond. Her mother and father tried explaining to her that she could not pick them, but Joanne still wanted to try. She thought that if she had a long stick, she would be able to get hold of one of them and pull it to the bank. But, the bank was slippery... Joanne fell into the water! Luckily, she was a good swimmer, but that did not stop her clothes getting soaked and muddy. And she did not have one Water-Lily to show for her trouble!

21 May

Looking rather sheepish, Joanne went home and told her mother.
"I only wanted to pick some Water-Lilies for my Aunt!" she began – but her mother did not want to hear. Joanne got a good scolding for being silly enough to go near water on her own. Then she was made to have a hot bath, followed by a drink of hot milk with honey.
"Next time," she thought, after being sent to bed early, "maybe I should pick some buttercups or daisies instead...."

22 May

The Picnic

It was a beautiful day, and Raymond, Amy and Isabel decided to have their lunch outdoors on the common.

"I'm taking the rolls!" said Amy.

"I'll fetch the milk!" added Isabel.

"And I'm bringing the fruit!" Raymond said.

So, the three of them set off, with the picnic food packed in a basket.

When they got to the common, the three friends came to a place where lots of mother sheep came with their lambs.

"Aren't they lovely?" cried Isabel.

"Look, I'm sure they're hungry!"

"Let's give them our rolls!" Amy suggested.

They quite enjoyed seeing the sheep and lambs eating their picnic lunch!

23 May

Soon afterwards, they came across some birds squabbling and squawking over an old apple core.

"Wait a minute!" cried Raymond. He took all the fruit out of the basket and gave it to them! "Now you won't have to argue!" he grinned.

Further on, at the edge of the common, something else made the three friends stop in their tracks.

"Oh!" cried Isabel. "What a dear little cat! Let's give it our milk, then we can take it home. Maybe we'll have an empty stomach, but we shall have made lots of friends!"

The Clouds

Did you know that a cloud is a mass of little drops of water up in the air? These drops come from the evaporation of sea water, and also from the fields and forests.

When there are too many drops for the cloud to hold, they fall as a light veil of drizzle, or a shower of rain.

And when there is a mist, do you know that you are walking through the heart of a big cloud?

Look at the clouds up in the sky. If you see the huge cumulus cloud, dark at the bottom and shaped rather like a blacksmith's anvil at the top, you will know that rain is on its way.

But if the clouds look white and fleecy, that is a sign of a beautiful day and fine weather.

24 May

25 May

The Obstacle Race

It is nice to get out, especially when we all know that fresh air and exercise is good for our health.

But what can you do when there isn't a park near where you live?

Well, you can always set up an obstacle course in the smallest garden with some jumping, crawling and climbing for you and your friends to do.

To begin with, try laying two lengths of rope or string on the ground a little way apart to make a pretend stream. Can you jump across it? Crawling under a chair, hopping or stepping between the rungs of ladder laid on the ground are some other easy ideas to try. And there are lots more!

26 May

What about using old newspapers to make stepping-stones?
Can you step or hop from one to the other without putting your feet on the ground? The further apart they are, the more difficult it gets!
Can you crawl under, or jump over a rope tied between two chairs?
Or walk around a chair with something on your head?
Try throwing a ball at a target, or see if you can get in a box.
These are just a few ideas which you could try wherever you live – and you're sure to think of lots more!

27 May

The Heron

One day, a heron made its way along the river bank, stepping slowly on its long, thin legs. It was a fine day and the bird's sharp eyes soon spotted a carp – a fish something like a pike – in the water. The heron knew he could take it without any trouble, but he thought it would be better to wait until he felt a bit hungrier. A heron eats only when he really wants to. Then he saw a tench swimming towards him, but he let that pass, too. He was waiting to get something much better.....

28 May

"A little tench is no meal for a fine heron like me!" he thought scornfully. But when the day passed without him seeing another single fish, the heron began to feel hungry. Night fell and he found himself wandering around the countryside looking for something to eat.

How he wished then that he had eaten such a splendid meal when he'd had the chance!

Now all he could find were a few bits of stale bread.

By wanting too much, that proud heron had lost everything.

29 May

The Goose Girl

There was once a young prince who loved nothing better than walking by himself in the forest.

One day he came across an old woman sitting wearily on a big rock. She had two heavy-looking baskets at her feet.

"I am so tired!" she told the prince. "Do you think you could carry me, just as far as my house?"

The kind young man did as the old woman asked and carried her home.

30 May

It was then the prince noticed a plain-faced girl looking after the geese.
The old lady thanked the prince and gave him a pearl. "This will bring you good fortune!" she told him.
And when the young prince returned to the palace and showed the pearl to his mother, the queen, she burst into tears. It was the pearl she had given to her baby daughter, who had vanished many years ago!
And whilst all this was happening, the old woman was telling the goose girl something equally strange...

31 May

"The prince's kindness has released you from an evil spell!" she told the girl. "Now, go and look into the fountain and you will see your beautiful face in the water!"
Meanwhile, the king and queen decided to go and see the old woman. On the way, they told the prince how they had lost their baby daughter, whilst out in the great forest.
And before long, the long-lost princess was returning to the palace with her mother and father, taking with her the old lady who had brought her up.

1 June

2 June

Then she went into the kitchen. On the table were three bowls of porridge – a big bowl, which was too hot, a medium sized bowl, which was too cold, and a tiny, little bowl which tasted so nice that Goldilocks soon ate it all up!

Now, feeling rather sleepy, she went up to the bedroom. Here, there were three beds – a big bed, which was too high, a medium-sized bed, which was too low, and a tiny, little bed, which was so comfortable that Goldilocks fell asleep. When she awoke, there were three bears looking at her!

Goldilocks and the Three Bears

There was once a little girl with such beautiful, curly, fair hair that everyone called her Goldilocks. What she liked best was to walk through the forest. No matter how often her parents told her not to go alone and to ask their permission, still she would go off on her long walks.

One day, she came across a little cottage she had not seen before. Goldilocks was so tired after her long walk and nobody seemed to be around. So, as the door was open a little, she went inside. It was all very quiet and tidy, with three chairs – a big chair which was too hard, a medium-sized chair, which was too soft, and a small chair, which Goldilocks thought was just right.

3 June

The bears were even more surprised than Goldilocks – although she did not know that. She was so frightened that she burst into tears.

Mummy Bear spoke gently to her. She told her that they had gone for a walk whilst their porridge cooled. When they said that they would show Goldilocks the way home, she dried her tears. They walked with her until her house came in sight, with her mother and father waiting. But no matter how many times she searched after that, she never did find the cottage of the three bears ever again.

4 June

The Card Party!

Uncle James was playing cards with all his nephews and nieces.
"The winner will get a nice prize!" he announced.
"What sort of prize?" asked Nancy, who always wanted to know everything.
"A medal!" he smiled. "Look!"
And they all admired the shining, gold medal and its long, coloured ribbon.
"I hope I win!" cried Garry, shuffling the cards.

5 June

All the players did their best. Uncle James wrote down who had won each game, then he added up the score. Roland was the winner. How the others scowled when Uncle James gave him the medal! All except Anne.

"Anne," said Uncle James, "here is your prize!"

And he gave her a lovely, big orange. "But, she didn't win any of the games!" protested Cilla.

"No," Uncle James agreed, "but she lost with a smile. And that's the main thing!"

6 June

The Flower Shops

Everyone loves flowers! And because they are so colourful to look at, lots of people like making them, too.

In many towns along the North Sea coast of Belgium, children have a contest every summer.

Beaches are transformed into parades of little shops, with paper flowers, which the children "sell" to other children for pebbles and shells.

Do you know how to make paper flowers?

7 June

First, find some scissors, thread or fine wire (fuse wire or a card of florist's wire is ideal) and scraps of crepe paper or plastic cut from carrier bags, and some drinking straws.

Cut the paper or plastic into long strips and wind these around the drinking straw. Then wind a piece of wire around the bottom of the plastic or paper to hold it firmly. You could try making different sorts of flowers – cut long, thin petal shapes for irises or a short fringe along one end for the shaggy chrysanthemum.

8 June

Frightened of Reptiles?

Snakes and lizards are both reptiles. If the weather is cold, then the lizard goes to sleep.

But when the sun shines, it is full of energy and very quick on its feet – as you will know, if you have ever tried to catch one!

Not only can the lizard move like lightning, it also has a very clever and unusual way of defending itself.

Because, if you try catching it by the tail, the tail just breaks off!

9 June

Why are people frightened of snakes? Perhaps it is because we so often hear bad things about them. But after we have watched them, very often the fear goes.

Two of the most common snakes are the grass snake and the viper – and it's important to know the difference. The grass snake is not poisonous, whereas the viper is.

The viper is smaller than the grass snake and has a triangular head. The grass snake has an oval head. Also, the grass snake will swim and climb trees, but the viper will not.

10 June

Where Did the Wild Strawberries Go?

"I'm going to pick some strawberries in the wood!" said Charlotte. "Can I take a basket from the cellar?"
She was looking forward to some strawberry picking! It was so hot that she tied a handkerchief around her head as protection against the sun – although filling the basket with strawberries did not take very long. But, was everything as perfect as it seemed?

11 June

If Charlotte had looked inside the basket when she found it in the cellar, she would have seen the little mouse whose home it was... And, as she carried the basket, so it rocked him to sleep! When he woke up, he felt very sleepy, and as fast as Charlotte filled the basket, so he emptied it!
But it was quite a while before she discovered what had been happening. "You villain!" she screamed at the mouse. "Now that you've had your share, I've a good mind to make you help me pick some more strawberries, tomorrow!"

12 June

Thoughts on Fathers' Day.

Fathers' Day will be coming soon.
But I do not have to wait for a special day to tell my Daddy I love him.
My Daddy is like a big brother to me. I can always talk to him about things which make me happy or sad, my hopes and dreams.
When I feel like crying, he tries to make me feel better.
I wish that all children in the world could have a father like mine.

13 June

The Hare and the Hounds

The month of June is the perfect time to play The Hare and the Hounds! It's a game which is a little like the story of Tom Thumb – where you have to find your way back home, following clues and signs along the way.

One group of players – The Hare – goes on ahead to lay these signs and clues. They can be twigs in the form of arrows, bits of wool or small balls of crumpled newspaper, which they put at "key places" for the other group of players – The Hounds. The Hounds have to follow the signs and find the The Hare (not forgetting to collect up all the signs on the way).

This is always a good game, and you can make it as easy or as difficult as you like.

14 June

How about leaving messages along the trail which players must follow to complete a course?

For example – find or bring back a hazel twig. Balance on a branch or a tree trunk to reach some hidden treasure or prize, etc.

It is always exciting to finish off the game with some sort of match between the two groups – a game of Hide-and-Seek, for example.

And it is always possible to introduce a theme to your game – Robin Hood, Red Indians... whatever you and your friends like best.

15 June

The Redcurrants

After doing their homework, Caroline and Sylvia love to go walking in the countryside near their home. One day, they noticed four magnificent old current bushes growing against the wall of a ruined manor house, with beautiful bunches of fruit ripening in the sun.

"Mmmmm!" murmured Sylvia. "Don't they look lovely?"

"Couldn't we have a taste?" said Caroline. And, without another word, they began picking great, big handfuls, cramming the fruit in their mouths as fast as they could!

"Mmmm, delicious!" declared Sylvia. They were both so busy eating the redcurrants, that they forgot their mother's advice, which was – always wash fruit before you start eating....

16 June

It was soon time to be getting back. Mummy and Daddy were waiting for the girls. But, as they reached home, Sylvia and Caroline both had tummy ache!

"What's wrong?" asked their mother. So, they just had to confess!

"We've eaten lots of redcurrants," said Caroline.

"And we didn't wash them..." added Sylvia.

"Then this will teach you a lesson!" their father scolded. "Instead of supper, you will have to be content with just a hot cup of tea!"

17 June

The Start of Hay-Making

John, the farmer, has a lot of work to do. The weather has been dry for a good fortnight, so now he has decided to start the hay-making.

"The grass is high!" John says to himself. "It's time I cut it down!" And so he fetches his tractor, ready to fix a mowing machine at the back.

"What are you going to do with all that grass, now it smells so nice?" asks Toby, getting off his bicycle and going over to get a closer look. He always likes to know what is happening!

"It's good grass for cattle," the farmer tells him. "When it is dry, I can tie it up in bundles, ready to be put in my hay loft. Then my cows will have plenty to eat all winter through. Would you like to help me stack the bundles tomorrow?"

18 June

Next day, when Toby goes to see Farmer John again, all the grass has been cut down, and the tractor now has a combine harvester fixed to the back. This machine picks up the grass and gathers it into bundles, which are then thrown out, all nicely tied up!

"Get a fork," the farmer tells Toby. "We'll start loading the hay on to the cart, ready to go into the hay loft!"

"But," puffs Toby, "it's so heavy!"

"In my grandfather's time," says Farmer John, "all this work was done by hand, not a machine! So I suppose we can think ourselves lucky!"

19 June

The Milkmaid and the Milk

There was once a young milkmaid, called Penny, who was going to town to sell her milk there.

It was a lovely day, and she took care to walk very carefully, the pot of milk on a little cushion which rested on her head.

All along the way, she kept thinking of the money she would get.

She could buy a hundred eggs, she decided, which would hatch into chickens and become hens, then she could sell their eggs!

After that, she thought, she would rear a few chickens in front of her house. Being able to run around would make them taste wonderful for a roast chicken dinner.

And when she sold those, what would she buy, next?

20 June

Perhaps a pig, she told herself! A pig would eat anything, so it would not cost much to keep. Then, when it was big and fat, she would sell it and buy a cow and her calf and watch them jumping about in the grass.

Quite forgetting herself, Penny jumped as well, and down fell the milk.

Calf, cow, pigs, chicks.... her fortune was gone. All she could do was to go back to the farm.

Penny knew then that it was unwise to make too many far-fetched plans. Day-dreamers always have to wake up!

Summer-Time!

Now it really is summer-time, the driest season of the year! The sun rises early and sets late in the day, making the days much longer and the nights shorter. No wonder so many of us like to get out in the fresh air! Do you know that the sun is a star, the nearest one to our earth? And the earth goes once around the sun each year, spinning on its own axis.

The part of the earth which is nearest the sun gets the most heat. And so, we get spring, when our part of the earth begins moving nearer the sun, then the summer, when it is really hot. Then, as we move away from the sun, we get less heat and it becomes autumn. And, as it gets colder and colder, so we have our winter.

21 June

22 June

Under Canvas

"It's summer-time!" Philip shouted to Alex. "It's warm enough to camp out!" "Great!" cried Alex. "Never mind about us not having a tent, we can soon make one!"

And they went to find some oil cloth for a ground sheet, a blanket to make a tent, and some broom handles for the tent posts.

Soon the house was being turned upside down! The two campers were determined to let nothing stop them! With an old eiderdown rescued from the attic to cover themselves, they went outside and got the tent up.

Just as they were thinking that they had nearly finished – disaster! There was a clap of thunder and it began to rain. Now, what could they do?

23 June

Feeling very proud of their handiwork, Philip and Alex hurried inside the tent! But it soon became clear that the tent was not waterproof!

"We're soaked already!" cried Philip. "We'd best go indoors – and quickly!"

"You're right!" Alex shouted back.

Luckily for them, their mother was a little wiser than her two sons.

She was waiting inside the house with bath towels and mugs of hot chocolate!

Nobody – grown-up or pretend Red Indian – could be quicker than that!

24 June

The Skylark

It was a really lovely summer morning, so Martin decided to go for a walk near his home. It all seemed very peaceful, but there was a lot of twittering and chirping in one part of the field. Martin looked all around, then raised his head.

"Now," he thought, "what is that bird who sings the whole time as it flies all the way towards the sun?"

Even when the bird was out of sight, Martin could still hear its song.

25 June

So, Martin went to ask Mr. Jones, the farmer.

"That's the skylark!" he said, when Martin told him. "Can you see the way it circles in the sky? Then when it has finished singing, it will dive straight back down to its nest, which it builds nearer the ground."

"French-speaking people call the skylark, 'Alouette'," Farmer Jones went on. "Have you heard the song 'Gentille Alouette' at all?" Martin nodded. "But I did not know what it was until now," he said.

26 June

The Brave Little Tailor

There was once a country which was terrorised by a wicked giant. At last, the king sent his knights to every public place with a proclamation. It said that whichever man killed the giant could marry his daughter, the princess.

But one little tailor heard nothing. He was too busy in his workshop, getting rid of all the flies. He had killed seven of them with one single blow!

27 June

The tailor felt very proud of himself. He went to the window and cried out, "Seven at one blow! I've just killed seven at one blow, all by myself! What a hero I am!"

Well, hearing all this, the king's guards took him to the palace at once where he was asked to repeat what he had said.

"I do not believe I am afraid of anything!" he ended, quite carried away by his story.

"Then," said the king, "as you are so brave, you can rid our land of this cruel giant!"

But, when the little tailor came face to face with the huge giant, he knew very well that he would never be strong enough to kill him!

As for the giant, when he saw the little tailor, he just burst out laughing.

28 June

"Not very big, are you?" he scoffed.

"Maybe not," said the man, "but I am the best tailor in the land!"

And, do you know what he did? He put his scissors up the giant's nose! The giant could do nothing! The tailor stitched and tied and cut and knotted, until the giant was completely bound up, unable to move at all. When the king heard what had happened, he brought the brave little tailor back to the palace and introduced him to his daughter.

And before long, the princess and the brave little tailor were married.

29 June

The School Party

The school term is drawing to a close, and so everyone is beginning to look forward to the holidays.

The Head Teacher wants the school to have a party, and today is the day. All the classes meet in the school gymnasium.

"We shall begin by playing a game of musical chairs!" announces old Mr. Graham, the history teacher. "And the person who wins the most games in each class, wins a record token!"

So, you can imagine all the smiles on the faces of the winners, when their names are announced!

"Good for you!" cry their class-mates. "Well done!"

"And now," says the Head Teacher when all the games are over, "shall we have some music?"

30 June

The children in the first year come up and sing the songs which they have been practising. Then there are songs for everyone to join in.

What a lovely day it is!

But all good things must come to an end and the children go back to their classes. Now it is time for reports to be given out! Will they be good? Or, bad? Everyone begins to wonder!

For some, there are smiles and cries of joy. For others, a few tears. But they all make up their minds to do their best when they return.

Now, it's the holidays!

1 July

It's Holiday Time!

This year, the Barber family are going to Portugal! It's a long way away, so Mr. Barber is taking his wife and his children by aeroplane.

"It's a dearer way to travel," he says, "but much faster and less tiring." Gemma and Colin are rather nervous. They have never been in an aeroplane before. And it seems they have so many questions which they want to ask their mother and father.

"Are people afraid of flying?"

"How many pilots are there?"

"Oh, do not worry about things like that," their mother smiles. "You will like it, you'll see!"

Grandfather is driving them to the airport. "Sure you have not forgotten anything?" he asks.

2 July

Mr. Barber registers their names and hands in their luggage, then they go on the moving carpet which will take them to the big aeroplane.

There is an air hostess to show them to their seats. "Fasten your safety belts," she says, as the engines start up.

The aircraft moves along the runway, Gemma and Colin holding their breath. It goes faster and faster, then the wheels leave the ground and the nose of the aircraft points up towards the sky, climbing higher and higher.

"We're flying!" cry the children.

3 July

Cinderella

There was once a girl whose mother died. When her father married again, it was to a woman who had two daughters of her own.

Her step-mother made the girl do all the housework, all the cooking, the cleaning and the washing, wearing only the oldest, most worn-out clothes. And because she spent so much time among the kitchen cinders, they called her Cinderella.

The woman's daughters were so ugly, they were known as the Ugly Sisters. They hated Cinderella because she was so kind and so pretty.

One day, there came news from the royal palace of a grand ball to be held in honour of the Prince Charming. Everyone was invited.

But, would Cinderella be able to go?

4 July

Cinderella's step-mother sent her to the kitchen, then had two beautiful gowns made for the Ugly Sisters. When it was time for the ball, Cinderella could not help crying into the cinders. That was when her Fairy Godmother arrived! With one tap of her magic wand, she dressed Cinderella in a lovely gown. Then she turned a pumpkin from the garden into a carriage, and six mice into six magnificent white horses. "You shall go the ball!" she told Cindrella. "But do not forget that my magic lasts only until the last stroke of midnight!"

5 July

Cinderella was so happy dancing with the handsome Prince Charming, that she quite forgot the time – until she heard the strokes of midnight chiming. She fled, losing one of her glass slippers, which the prince picked up. "The girl whose foot this slipper fits, will be my wife," he said. Well, all the maidens of the kingdom tried it on, with the Ugly Sisters hoping it would fit them! But, of course, as soon as the prince saw Cinderella put the slipper on her dainty, little foot, he knew she was girl at the ball, the one he loved.

6 July

Summer Fruit

Marcus and Sally's favourite summer fruit is the cherry! Near their home is a lovely, big cherry tree which is always heavy with fruit. Sally loves picking them to make ear-rings, or helping Marcus to fill a basket with enough for a cherry pie, a fruit salad and lots of other lovely things!

"Hurry up, Sally!" cries Marcus. "We don't want the birds eating the cherries before we've had our share!"

7 July

Summer Night Hunting......

Holiday time! And nobody likes going to bed early on summer nights, do they? But, Cathy had an idea....
"What about going on a moth hunt tonight?" she suggested to Tom and Nicholas, her two cousins.
"Sounds great!" cried Tom, always ready to try anything different. "I'll go and get my torch."
But Nicholas did not seem quite so enthusiastic. He was younger than Cathy and Tom, and he did not much like the dark. But he tried to put a brave face on things and went to get a jar and his butterfly net.
"Don't forget!" said Cathy's Mum, as they all set off. "Stay together and keep within sight of the house, where we can see you from the window!"

8 July

Cathy's Dad also had a little orchard at the bottom of the garden.
But just as the three friends were busy exploring, the torch began flickering.
"The battery must be dead!" cried Nicholas. He was very frightened.
"Now, what are we going to do?"
Just then, Tom gave a whisper.
"Look! Glow-worms! Let's catch some in our jar!"
"Aren't they lovely?" smiled Nicholas, quite forgetting how frightened he was. "Never mind moths! I like glow-worms much better!"

9 July

Birds of Prey

Because birds of prey always look so fierce and menacing, we often suspect them of doing lots of damage.

In fact, these birds are very useful to us, even though their cries and their sharp beaks and claws can make us feel afraid at times.

Jason loves to watch one of these magnificent birds – the buzzard. Some people call it the flying stag, because of the way it stretches its wings out, making them look like antlers.

The sharp eyes of the buzzard mean that it can see the tiniest bird, field mouse or baby rabbit.

The buzzard hunts in daylight, like the sparrow-hawk and the falcon. But other birds of prey hunt at night.

And none of them are omens of bad luck, as many people often think.

10 July

"Twit-Twoo! Twit-Twoo!"
An owl hoots through the night.
He is another very useful bird of prey who feeds on insects and other harmful creatures.

And, like other birds of prey, the owl spits out little pellets made up of the uneaten bits which it cannot digest – such as bones, feathers and fur. You can often find these pellets at the bottom of a fir-tree or even in a barn. Break open the pellet – and you will discover a lot about the eating habits of this bird of prey.

11 July

The Hungry Seagulls!

Nancy and Abigail were spending a few days at the seaside.

Early each morning, they set off with their daddy, taking the dog for a walk along the beach before it got too hot. There were always lots of gulls flying around, crying and squawking as they searched for food. "Let Pepsi off the lead," said Daddy. "He could do with a run!"

And, as the dog ran towards the gulls, they flew off with a series of squawks, returning in a few strokes of the wing.

"What do they eat?" asked Nancy.

"Mussels, crabs, bread, shrimps..." Daddy told her.

"So, can we throw them some bread and butter?" asked Abigail.

12 July

Abigail had brought a few slices of bread with her.

"All right!" smiled Daddy. "Let's give them a treat!"

The girls soon broke the bread and butter into pieces, throwing them for the gulls to eat.

With another burst of squawking and crying, the birds swooped down for their breakfast. They made such a noise that Nancy and Abigail were a bit frightened and pressed close to their Daddy. "Yes, the gulls are hungry this morning!" he laughed.

13 July

A Fishing Line.....

"What?" Sam's Dad was saying. "You've never been fishing, so now you want to try it?"
Sam had been watching a television programme about fishing.
"Well, that's easily settled!"
"But don't I need anything?" asked Sam.
"You've got some rubber boots and an old anorak or mackintosh, haven't you?" said his father. "You don't need anything too grand!"
"What about a fishing rod?"
"Don't worry! A string tied on the end of a stick, a cork, a weight and a hook with some bait, and you're ready to start!"
Sam was delighted. He could already see himself catching a fine, big fish on the end of his line!

14 July

Sam and his Dad were soon out fishing, watching the line very carefully.
"It takes a long time," said Sam at last, a bit tired of waiting. "Do we need any more bait on the line?"
Dad did not say anything. At the end of the line, he had seen a slight movement in the water, which Sam had not yet noticed.
Suddenly, he cried out, "Pull hard, son! Hey, what about that? It's a fine, little trout!"
Sam could not get over it! Already he had forgotten how long he had waited for his first catch!

Leap Frog!

Carole quite liked the cool, damp mornings, when she could put on her dungarees and explore the grounds of the hotel, where she was staying with her parents.

"They've got a fishing contest here today," she told them. "And I saw some ducks, water-lilies..."

"And what have you got in your pocket?" asked her father.

"Only a frog!" grinned Carole, and put it on the dining room table.

The frog looked so funny, jumping over the plates then down on to the floor!

All the waiters tried to catch the frog. Some of the ladies screamed out in fright......

And, the children? They laughed until the tears rolled down their faces!

15 July

16 July

Ali-Baba and the Forty Thieves

One day, a poor man called Ali-Baba was journeying home on his donkey, when he heard the noise of horses galloping up behind him.

Feeling rather frightened, he got down from the donkey and hid behind some rocks, just moments before forty men appeared, all carrying heavy sacks.

"Open Sesame!" cried one – and the rock slid back to reveal the opening of a cave!

And when the men had carried all the sacks inside, the same man said, "Close, Sesame!" Then the rock slid back, and the men rode off.

So, Ali-Baba went to the same spot and said the same words. "Open, Sesame!" And the rock slid back.

17 July

He found the most wonderful store of precious stones, gold, jewels... every possible kind of treasure! Ali-Baba filled a sack and went out again – not forgetting to close the door.

Back home, he could not help telling his brother, Cassim, about it all.

But when Cassim went to the cave, he was captured by the forty thieves and killed.

Next time Ali-Baba went to the cave, he found Cassim's body and took his dead brother back home. This told the forty thieves that a second person knew of their secret hiding place! And because Ali-Baba was Cassim's brother, a member of the band followed him and saw where he lived. A few days later, a merchant came and asked Ali-Baba if he could leave forty jars of oil in his yard until the next day....

18 July

Morgana, the servant girl, was sure that the thieves were hiding in the jars. By night-fall, she had boiled up lots of water, then poured it into the jars! The forty thieves had perished even before they had time to cry out! And when the gang leader came back and found that his men had been killed, he fled – whilst Morgana watched the yard, ready to signal to Ali-Baba.

All the treasures in the cave were sold and the money given to the poor. Then Ali-Baba and the faithful Morgana were married, loved and respected by all the people.

19 July

On the Harvester

This year, with the spears of corn gleaming like gold in the sunshine, Mr. Cornford, the farmer, has said tha Ralph can help him on the combine harvester.

There is a roar of sound as he starts up the engine. Then the blades begin turning, cutting down the corn, ready to go into a threshing machine to separate the grains from the "chaff" or pieces of straw.

All sorts of insects can be seen flying around in front of the terrible jaws of the metal monster!

As for the animals and birds – rabbits, pheasants and partridges run for their lives!

20 July

Suddenly, Ralph gives a shout. "Stop, Mr. Cornford!" And he climbs down from the cab and dashes in front of the harvester, kneeling down to pick up something. Can you think what it is? Yes, it's a hedgehog!

"What are you going to do with that?" Farmer Cornford wants to know. "It's only a baby!"

"Yes," says Ralph, "but if I take it home and keep it in our vegetable garden, it will eat all the insects and slugs! Much better than being out here in the cornfield!"

Buzzing in the Ears!

"Paul isn't up, yet!" Mum said to Dad one morning. "And that isn't like him at all. Can you go up to him and see if there is anything wrong?"

"What's the matter, son?" asked Dad, going into Paul's bedroom.

"I don't know," said Paul, "but I must be ill. My ears are buzzing all the time!"

"Then I'd best call the doctor," said Dad. "Buzzing in the ears can be serious!"

And, yet – it did not seem to him as if Paul had a cold or anything like that. So, what could be causing this strange buzzing in the ears? Only the doctor would be able to tell.....

But even the doctor seemed rather puzzled.

"You do not have a temperature," he told Paul. "It is all very strange." Suddenly, the doctor stood quite still. Then he went towards the window. It was a warm day, so he opened it wide.

And he, too, heard buzzing in the ears!

"The solution to the mystery is here!" he said, beginning to laugh. "There is a wasp's nest in the corner! Call the workmen, Paul! They will cure you much quicker than me!"

23 July

Glow-Worms and Fireflies

It was a hot summer night, and so Susan and David and their parents decided to try some of the "night life" in the country.

Armed with a pocket torch, the four of them began exploring the darkened undergrowth – although Susan did not much like the mosquitoes buzzing around her!

Suddenly, they all saw a little speck of light, shining as brightly as a star falling from the sky....

"That's a glow-worm!" Daddy told Susan and David. "Don't touch it, though. The slightest movement and it will disappear!"

Daddy told them something else. The glow-worm is not a worm at all, but an insect with wings!

24 July

Susan and David really liked watching the glow-worms.

"I'd like to be able to glow like that," David said to his sister. "Then I wouldn't have to carry a torch!"

"And I would never be afraid of the dark!" added Susan.

There were some other lights flitting around bushes, a little further on. These were fireflies, their pretty, sparkling lights seeming to dance in the darkened wood – like little people carrying torches, Susan thought!

25 July

The Stars in Summer

Summer is a good time to look at the stars shining in the night sky.

Stars are great balls of fiery gasses. We see them as small objects because they are millions and millions of miles away from us.

It's easy to learn how to recognise the stars.

In summer, you can easily see a great, silvery trail, made up of millions of stars and stretching across the sky. This is the Milky Way.

Another star formation, which is just as easy to see, is the Great Bear. This is made up of seven stars in the shape of a big cart – which is why it is also called The Plough.

Or, look out for the one star which is set apart from the others and shines the brightest in the sky. This is the North Star.

26 July

"Look at that star going across the sky!" cried Kim. "It's all bright and shining, as if it's on fire!"

You can often see these "shooting stars" when the sky is clear.

Do not mistake them for an aeroplane, which travels much more slowly.

In fact, these "shooting stars" are not stars at all, but fragments of rock which travel through space, bursting into flames as they come into contact with the atmosphere.

Whenever you see a shooting star, be sure to make a wish! It is supposed to come true...

27 July

Treasure Hunting!

What do you think you could make with the shells, or the pretty stones and pebbles, you can collect on the beach? There are plenty of ideas you could try!

A little hole made at the top of a shell will make it into something nice to wear – a pendant to thread on a string, or a badge on to a safety pin. Or, you could try building shells into a little man, or perhaps funny animals. Can you find a piece of cardboard or wood? If so, then you could also try sticking shells onto it with glue, to make shell pictures or patterns.

When your work is finished, see if you can cover it with a coat of clear varnish. It will last longer, then!

28 July

Have you ever thought of using shells and pebbles as draughts or chequers on the beach?

It's so easy to mark out a game of draughts or hopscotch on the sand! Or, what about an indoor game?

Make your pebbles and shells into a treasure trove, painting or decorating them to look like precious stones and jewels.

Then hide the treasure around the house and whoever finds the most treasure, to fill a treasure chest, is the winner!

29 July

The Lion and the Rat

The lion was feeling very pleased with life! He had just eaten a good meal. Now, he was settling down for a nice, comfortable snooze.

He was in a very good mood. Suddenly, the ground trembled! Before the lion's eyes, the earth rose up and a hole appeared, closely followed by a fine pair of whiskers!

It was a rat – quite astonished to find himself between the paws of a great lion. The rat's life was now in great danger. Only one false move, he knew, and he would be no more.

But the lion, king of the beasts, was quite amused by the little creature who had disturbed his rest.

He invited the rat to go walking with him!

30 July

The rat was so glad to think he was still alive, that he thanked the lion and they went off together.

The lion had spared the life of the rat. But the rat was about to save the life of the lion. Because, as they walked a little further, the lion, big and strong, was caught in a net. But the rat ran quickly away.

Then, with his sharp little teeth, the rat gnawed and nibbled until he had chewed through just one stitch – and the whole net came undone!

Which shows that patience can often succeed where strength fails.

Duck to the Rescue!

Baby Alex had been given two lovely presents for his birthday – a big, furry bear and a blue duck on wheels. So far, Alex could only walk a few steps on his own. Then he got tired and had to sit down. That was when he picked up the bear. He squeezed him very hard, or pulled his hair, or threw him against the legs of the table, hugging him hard, then twisting his head!

"Poor Bruno the bear!" thought Quack, the wooden duck. "I think I shall last a little longer with baby. I am more solid than a furry bear."

Then, with one last pull on Bruno's paw, baby Alex laid down and went to sleep.

His Mummy laid him in his cot, then put his other toys away in a big box.

"I would like to help you, Bruno," said Quack, rolling towards the bear and seeing all the loose stitches and gaping holes. "I'm quite handy with my needle, you know!"

And he stitched and sewed, repairing all the damage Alex had done, with a needle and some strong, brown thread.

"Thank you, Quack!" said Bruno. "I feel much better, now! Oh, that baby... he can be cruel!"

"But he is so beautiful when he's asleep!" admitted Quack. "Ssssh, don't make a noise!"

And the two toys went quietly to the cot to look at the sleeping baby, thumb in his mouth, a lovely smile on his little face.

"You're right, Quack!" whispered Bruno. "He's just like an angel...."

1 August

Returning Home

Barbara and Gregory had been on holiday with their mother and father for the whole of July – swimming, sunbathing, playing on the beach... So, when they returned home, they were all looking very brown.

Mummy was a little worried because Grandma had not been very well. So, as soon as they had unpacked their suitcases, the family went to see her. They were all pleased to find Grandma looking better than they had expected.

"And how are my grandchildren?" she smiled, very pleased to see them. Gregory went and flung his arms around her neck. "Gently does it, Gregory!" laughed Daddy. "You don't want to hurt Grandma! "But Grandma only smiled at him. Then she said to Mummy, "and who is this little girl you've brought to see me?"

This is Barbara!" Mummy laughed, pretending to be surprised.

"Yes, it's me!" cried Barbara, throwing her arms around Grandma's neck. Soon, Grandma felt as though she couldn't take in all the news they had to tell her!

2 August

Little Red Riding Hood

Little Red Riding Hood was a kind little girl, who got her name because of the red cape and hood which she always wore when she went out.

One day, she set off to visit her Grandma, who was ill. The old lady lived in a house on the edge of the forest. On the way, Little Red Riding Hood met a wolf.

"Where are you going?" he asked Red Riding Hood.

"To see my Grandma," she smiled. "I'm taking her a few things, because she is not very well."

Hearing this, the wolf took a short cut so that he would reach the old woman's cottage before Red Riding Hood! Knock-Knock! He rapped at the door.

"Who is there?" called a voice.

3 August

"It's Little Red Riding Hood!" cried the wolf, making his voice sound as sweet as he could.

Grandma sensed there was something wrong. She just managed to hide inside a big cupboard before the wolf came in. Seeing nobody there, he got into bed and waited for Little Red Riding Hood to arrive.

No wonder Red Riding Hood thought her Grandma looked rather different! "Oh, Grandma!" she said. "What big teeth you have!"

"All the better to eat you with!" roared the wolf, leaping out of bed.

4 August

"Help!" screamed Red Riding Hood. "Help! The wolf is going to get me!" All at once, Grandma burst out of the cupboard and gave the wolf such a big whack on his head with her rolling pin! He just had enough strength left to go off into the forest and run away as far as he could!

"All this has made me hungry!" said Little Red Riding Hood.

"Me, too!" smiled Grandma. And together they laid the table, ready to eat all the goodies in Red Riding Hood's basket.

5 August

The Old Apple Tree

Once upon a time on this day, the wind chanced to stop in Caroline's garden.

"What is wrong?" he asked the old apple tree there. "You're looking so miserable!"

"That's because I'm getting old!" answered the tree in its weak, groaning sort of voice. "My branches are so heavy, weighed down by all these apples!"

"Don't worry!" whistled the wind. "I shall soon help you!"

6 August

The wind took a long, deep breath, then blew hard with all his might. "Ow-ow!" groaned the old apple tree, even before a single apple fell to the ground. "You're hurting me!"
The wind wondered what he could do next. Then, very quietly, he crept in among the branches of the old apple tree. And, as if by magic, the delicious scent of fruit filled the air and drifted through the window into Caroline's bedroom!
"Mmmm!" she said. "That smells lovely! I think I'll go and pick some of those apples!"

7 August

The Honey-bee and the Daisy

Bumble, the honey-bee, loved all the flowers in the garden, but the daisy was his favourite.
"What's the news today?" he said. "Have you got any nice nectar for me?"
"Just as long as you do not tickle me too much!" smiled Daisy.
"Mmmm...." said Bumble, "do you know, your nectar is the best for miles around? It's all thanks to you that we make such good honey! Would you like to know how we make it?"

8 August

"Well," Bumble went on, "after I've been here, I go back to the hive!"
"And is it true that you dance?" Daisy interrupted.
"Well," said Bumble again, "I fly in circles and I hum, to show other bees where the nicest flowers are. Then I put my nectar in the honeycomb of the Queen Bee, so that she can make honey."
"Would you let me taste the honey?" Daisy asked her friend.
"Of course," buzzed Bumble, "but the honey is not meant for us! It's to give to children and grown-ups for them to enjoy!"

9 August

The Campers Return Home!

Derek, Robert and Larry have all spent a week camping in the woods with the Scouts.
Now, their stay is over and so the Scout Master brings them home in his range rover.
"You're all muddy and dirty!" says Mum. "We couldn't wash ourselves too well!" Robert tells her.
"And why was that?" Mum wants to know.

10 August

"Because the water in the river was too cold!" says Larry. "Phew!" says Dad, holding his nose. "No wonder you're all a bit smelly!"
"Good Scouts should always have a good wash," scolds Mum, "even if the water is cold! What you need now is a nice, hot bath with plenty of soap!"
"Doesn't sound a bad idea to me!" grins Derek.
"Worth getting nice and dirty for!" adds Larry.
And even Mummy and Daddy have to laugh.

11 August

A Pretty Picture

Robin's grandfather has asked him to help sort out his tool shed. "Great!" says Robin, always pleased to help Grandpa.
But, as he goes into the shed, he quickly steps back.
"Ugh!" he cries. "It's full of spiders' webs!"
"What's wrong with spiders' webs?" smiles Grandpa. "Maybe you do not know enough about them, that's all. Listen, and I'll tell you something....."

12 August

"When I was small," the old man goes on, "I spent a lot of time watching spiders. Sometimes, I used a magnifying glass. Other times, I would pick a blade of grass to set them trembling in the web!"

"Go and fetch your Mummy's hair-spray!" Grandpa continues. "We'll spray it on a web, then put it under a sheet of glass. You just wait and see what a work of art a spider's web really is!"

"You're right, Grandpa!" cries Robin. "I would never have thought it!"

13 August

Something Made of Wood

Olivia, Rosie and Clive were helping their Daddy to set up a barbecue.
"I need quite a few pieces of wood," he told them. "Bring me back whatever you can find."
Well, as there were three of them, it was quite easy to find the wood they wanted. In fact, the children brought back so much wood that Daddy found he had far more than he needed! Something had to be done. The wood was blocking up the whole garden!

14 August

Then, Daddy had an idea.
"Follow me, children!" he said, leading the way to the bottom of the garden. And soon all the wood they had collected was stacked up neatly and covered with plastic to keep it dry. Of course, the three children wanted to know what Daddy's idea was!
"What about your own hut in the garden?" he said at last. "That's if you can find some more wood!" "Terrific!" they cried.
"Just what we need!" added Clive, as they went to start searching again.

15 August

Aladdin and the Wonderful Lamp

Once upon a time, in a far-off land, there was a poor young man called Aladdin, who lived with his mother. One day, an old man called on them and said that he was Aladdin's Uncle. But, he was a wicked magician.
He took Aladdin into the desert and told him to make a fire.
Then, as the magician threw some magic powder into the flames, the ground opened up to reveal a cave!

16 August

"Take this ring," said the magician. "It will protect you from the genies in the cave! Now, go and bring me the oil lamp you will see down there!"

What a sight there was inside the cave – precious stones, gold... Aladdin looked for so long that the magician grew impatient and closed the entrance to the cave as a punishment! Aladdin was frightened. Without thinking, he rubbed the lamp – and a genie appeared, asking what he wanted!

Aladdin filled a chest with precious stones and said he wanted to return home. In just a few seconds, his wish was granted, and he was telling his mother all that had happened.

Thanks to genie granting his wishes whenever he rubbed the lamp, Aladdin soon became rich enough to marry the daughter of the Sultan.

17 August

When the magician heard of Aladdin's good fortune, he made up his mind to get the lamp. It was when Aladdin returned from his latest journey and saw that the magic lamp was missing, that he remembered the ring which the magician had given him.

One turn of the ring on his finger, and another genie appeared, ready to take Aladdin to the magic lamp!

Soon, he had the lamp, and had beaten the magician, so that he and the Sultan's daughter could live happily, loved by everyone in their kingdom.

18 August

The Greenfly and the Ladybird

In summer-time, when it is really hot, there are often swarms of little greenfly all over the rose bushes, around the stems and on the leaves, not worrying at all about the prickly thorns!

One greenfly was gently tickling one of the rose petals where he had been for most of the day. And, as he was feeling very full, he decided to have a nice rest.

"Ah," he thought, leaning back comfortably, "it's a good life, here!" He felt very happy as he fell asleep. But that greenfly was not very clever. He had decided to take a rest, when hunters were getting nearer every minute....

19 August

It so happened that a ladybird flew down on to the rose bush. Gently, she closed her wings and began climbing up from one stalk to the next.

"Ooh, I'm so hungry!" she thought to herself, seeing some of the little creepy-crawlies which would make a very good meal, indeed!

By now, the greenfly had woken up, listening. Sensing the danger, he pushed a drop of rose-water, so that it slid down on top of the ladybird, making her go somewhere else for her dinner!

20 August

21 August

And as they fished, so Scott kept
count.

"That's the fourth trout we've caught!"
he cried – just as Candy, their cocker
spaniel, came up to the two fishermen.
To show how pleased she was to see
them, she wagged her tail so hard,
that she bumped into the bucket. Over
it went, sending their hopes of trout for
lunch back into the water.

"Oh, no!" groaned Scott, clutching his
head.

"These things happen!" smiled Dad.
"We'll have fun, catching them
again!"

The Fishing Trip

The Bramley family were camping on
the banks of a river.

Early each morning, Scott and his
father left the caravan to go fishing for
trout.

Freshly fried fish, with salt, pepper,
parsley, a twist of lemon and brown
bread! Mmmm! No wonder it was the
family's favourite lunch!

"Don't just sit there thinking about
eating the fish," laughed Dad, getting
his fishing rod ready. "We've got to
catch them first!"

"We'll soon do that!" grinned Scott,
sounding very sure of himself. "You'll
see, Dad!"

And, all went well.

The trout took the bait and were easily
caught. Then they were taken off the
hook and put into a bucket of water.

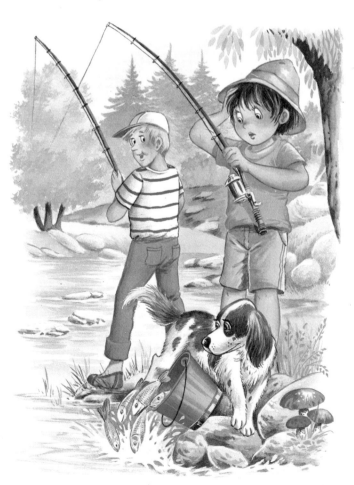

22 August

Mushroom Picking

"Shall we go mushroom picking tomorrow, Paul?" Sharon said to her brother. "It's very warm and muggy this evening, so there should be plenty!"

"All right," agreed Paul. "Do you know where we can go?"

"Of course I do!" grinned Sharon. "You know the field where Mrs. Joseph takes her cows to graze? Well, it's the perfect spot for mushroom picking!"

"Maybe...." sighed Paul, not seeming quite so pleased. "But couldn't we find a field with a horse instead of a cow?"

"Trust me!" smiled Sharon. "Just go to bed, now – and remember to get up early tomorrow!"

23 August

By daybreak next morning, Sharon and Paul were ready. Wearing their rubber boots and carrying a big basket between them, they made their way to Mrs. Joseph's field.

"We'll rake over the grass, bit by bit!" Sharon told Paul. "You go over that side, and I'll look just here."

"Oh, look!" cried Paul. "A whole clump of mushrooms! You hold the basket, Sharon!"

"No," Sharon said firmly. "Those aren't the sort we can eat. Look, they don't have any tails! They're toadstools!"

24 August

The Pigeon and the Ant

There was once a pigeon who liked nothing better than splashing in the waters of a stream.

One day, an ant who happened to be passing that way, fell in.

Bravely, the ant tried to swim to the bank, but it was quite hopeless.

The waters of the stream were like a giant ocean to the tiny creature.

Now, the pigeon, busy having a drink, saw that the little insect was about to drown. He wanted to help the ant. But, how?

Suddenly, the bird picked a blade of grass and drew it across the surface of the water, near enough to the ant for him to reach it, walk along it, and on to dry land once more.

25 August

The pigeon made sure that the ant was safe and sound.

Then he noticed a man, walking along quietly, holding a shot-gun.

The pigeon did not trust him – and with good cause. He was already seeing a hot pigeon pie on his table. He raised his gun and took aim. But the ant, seeing that the pigeon was in danger, stung the man on the ankle, making the gun go off by accident. And, as the pigeon flew to safety, he could not help thinking how useful the tiniest of creatures could often be to those much bigger than themselves.

26 August

The Sandman Brings Dream

Natalie was about to fall fast asleep! She vaguely remembered hearing about the Sandman bringing wonderful dreams...

Would he be taking her off to his wonderful home at the seaside? What would it be like?

Suddenly, as if she had been blown there on a puff of wind, she found herself on a warm, sandy beach, with lots of other children, all having a lovely time!

"Come and play with me!" one of them called. "Look, I'm drawing something in the sand, and you have to guess what it is!"

"No!" someone else was saying. "Let's go a bit further this way. Then we can have a sand-castle competition!"

27 August

It was a wonderful place to be! "Those children look funny over there!" she thought, watching them all walking backwards over a line of shells.

Some others had made a throwing game with beach balls and buckets. Natalie could not help clapping!

"This is the best playground there ever was!" she told herself. "It's like a beautiful dream!" Perhaps Natalie was only dreaming. But she had lots of ideas for holiday games to play when she woke up!

28 August

The Potato Harvest

"Let's spend the last few days of the holidays digging up the potatoes!" said Daddy.

"Yes, let's!" nodded Ben, the eldest. "What do you think, Philip?"

"All right!" he grinned.

And so the hard work began. Daddy dug up the potatoes and as the two boys watched, he put them in buckets. Soon, Ben was bringing his two buckets of potatoes to the house, putting them on the tiles of the patio. But Philip was trailing quite a way behind his brother, and the reason was quite unusual....

29 August

On the fourth trip back to the house, Mum brought out some lemonade. At that very same moment, Philip caught his foot in a rake, and over went the buckets he was carrying. That was when Mum saw that the two buckets were only half full.

Philip had put crumpled-up newspaper underneath the potatoes!

"You cheat!" Mum scolded. "Fancy doing a thing like that!"

"And now," said Dad, "you can carry on until you have done your fair share of the work!"

30 August

Journeying Home

Roger, Cathy, Mark and their parents were coming back home after a lovely holiday at the seaside.

"I love going on the train!" declared Cathy, looking out at the scenery.

"We're due to arrive at ten o'clock, tomorrow!" said Daddy with a smile. "So I think we'll have something to eat, then it's bed time!"

"I'm not tired!" said Mark, trying not to yawn. "But I do feel hungry!"

But shortly after the meal was over, the children had fallen asleep – not in their beds, but on the bunks of the sleeping car.

Next morning, they could see Grandma and Grandpa waiting for them on the platform, as Daddy collected up all the luggage from the sleeping car.

31 August

"There's no rush!" said Daddy. "Wait until the train stops before going out into the corridor!"

There was only one problem as they got off.

Roger, Cathy and Mark were just giving Grandma and Grandpa a hug, when Roger gave a shout.

"My shells! I left them in the carriage!"

But, it was too late. The train was pulling out.

"Don't worry!" said Mummy. "When we go back next year, there will be lots more for you to collect and more beautiful than before!"

1 September

Back to School!

The big day has arrived! Once again, the children are on their way to school. The juniors are meeting up with their friends. The infants walk more slowly into the playground.

A few in the "baby class" want to hold Mummy or Daddy's hand, trying to keep back the tears.

Those with a big brother or sister are slightly less anxious. They know that they will meet up again at playtime. All too soon the whistle blows, and everyone gets into lines.

Now, there may be some crying, because the little ones have to leave Mummy and Daddy and go with somebody they do not know. What will happen next, they wonder?

2 September

First, teacher gives out some lovely, new exercise books, rulers and pencils.

Then she gets to know everyone, asking them all about their holidays and the things they have done.

The "old hands" set to work, writing their names on the front of their exercise books, then giving out books and the paper to cover them with.

In no time at all, it is twelve o'clock! Mums and Dads are already waiting at the gate, ready to ask their children about the first morning at school.

3 September

Thumbelina

There was once an old woman who was so sad because she did not have any children. Then, one morning, in the heart of a flower, she found a tiny, little girl! As the girl was no bigger than the old woman's thumb, she decided to call her Thumbelina.

One night, a huge toad found Thumbelina asleep. "She will make a fine wife for my son!" he thought. So he carried her to a pond and put her on a water-lily.

Next morning, Thumbelina burst into tears. That was when the fish said that all the tiny creatures would help her. A butterfly pulled the leaf to the bank and a mayfly set her down in the meadow. And so, Thumbelina spent the summer, eating nectar and drinking dew from the flowers.

But summer would not last for ever.....

4 September

When winter came, Thumbelina was so hungry and cold, with only a dead, shrivelled-up leaf to cover herself. Then, she met a mouse who invited Thumbelina to live with her. And in return, Thumbelina did the cooking and the housework.

One day, on her way to see their neighbour, Mr. Mole, she found an injured swallow.

"I'll take care of you!" she cried, covering up the poor bird, already half dead with cold. How glad she was when its heart began beating again!

5 September

Under Thumbelina's care, the swallow soon got better, flying away when spring came. Now, Thumbelina's life was sad again – sadder still when Mr. Mole asked her to marry him. She hated the idea of living under the ground.

Out she went to say farewell to the sun and the flowers.

"Come with me!" came the voice of the swallow. "I'll take you to the land of sunshine!"

And in this country, Thumbelina met an elf who asked her to marry him. How happy she was to be the wife of such a kind, cheerful little man!

6 September

Pears to Cook!

Darren and Sandra picked some green pears and brought them home to their mother.

"Thank you!" she smiled. "We cannot eat these pears now, but I'll cook them for tea!"

"Will they be soft and sweet?" asked Darren.

"Of course!" smiled his mother. "Now, hurry up, otherwise you'll be late!"

"Goodbye, Mum!" they called, each wondering what the cooked pears would taste like.....

7 September

When it was time for tea, Sandra and her brother sat down at the kitchen table. Then their mother gave them each a great big pear, gleaming with syrup and brown sugar!

They soon got their teeth into a treat like that!

"Mmmm, great!" cried Darren.

"Delicious!" added Sandra.

In fact, they were so busy eating those pears, they got syrup all over their chins, noses, hands, and cheeks.

"Mmmmm!" Darren and Sandra said again, taking another mouthful.

"You're a terrific cook, Mum!"

8 September

A Surprise Picking!

It was the blackberry picking season! Karen and Steven's Mummy and Daddy said that tomorrow they could go off to the woods.

But, next day, they were going along a little country lane, when the car broke down! All Daddy could do was to go and try to get some help!

The children were left to wander around. Their Mummy said they just might find some blackberries to pick, after all....

9 September

But the only blackberries were behind the hedges all along the lane!
Karen and Steven were very, very disappointed.
"Don't say we've got to go home empty-handed!" said Karen.
"Open your eyes!" smiled Mummy. "There are dozens of hazel trees all around, with hazelnuts just right for picking!"
And so, all thoughts of making blackberry jam were set aside for another day.
But, the hazelnuts? What a delicious treat they were!

10 September

What a Lovely Little Village!

Mushrooms in the autumn woodland come in all shapes and all sorts of different colours – little, round, yellow ones; violet, trumpet-shaped ones; short, fluffy ones.... a whole, little village of mushroom houses!
And if you look long and hard, each one seems to have a little, tiled roof. People say that this is where the elves live.....

11 September

"Welcome to Flypaper Town!" calls one of the little elves. "I am the Mayor, and this is my friend, Mr. Martin, the carpenter, who keeps our little houses in good repair! Then there is our chief cook, Mr. Barker."

"We call our home Flypaper Town because we do not like to be disturbed by flies! We sleep through the day, which is why nobody ever sees us around. It is at night-time that we like to go out, gathering up all the flies for the birds to eat!"

"And some people think that we only exist in fairy stories!"

12 September

Let Battle Commence!

This evening, in the heart of the wood, the animals are all of a flutter. Soon, in the clearing, there is going to be a battle – a battle between two stags. Nigel and his Dad are perched high up on the observation platform, waiting patiently.

Suddenly, a loud cry echoes through the wood. "Don't be frightened, Nigel!" says his father. "That's only the sign that the battle is about to start! Look, the herd is coming…. Sssh, not a sound, now….."

13 September

The does and the young fawns stand around in a circle, whilst the two stags sharpen their antlers.

"Why are they battering against each other?" whispers Nigel.

"Because the winner will be the head of the herd!" his father tells him.

And so, the duel begins.

Heads lowered, the two stags lock antlers and start wrestling against each other.

"Fortunately," says Nigel's Dad,"they know when to stop. A stag is never killed when the leader of the herd is decided."

14 September

Star-watching

"Next weekend," Mr. Johns told his class, "I want you all to come to my house, so that we can look at the stars through my telescope!"

Mr. Johns never made any jokes, so, when he said that he wanted his class to do something, none of them could refuse.

The nights are clear in this month of September, and as the days are short, nobody in Mr. Johns' class went to bed very late. But, first they had to learn the names of the stars.

15 September

Well, the weekend arrived. The children were a bit annoyed about having a lesson in the evening, in the dark, and having to look up at the sky. And, of course, they had to pay attention, because Mr. Johns always asked them questions, afterwards. Then, just as the teacher was getting the telescope ready – CRASH! There was a loud clap of thunder! "Quick!" cried Mr. Johns. "Everyone inside! The stars will have to wait for another time!"

They all sat and drank a cup of hot chocolate instead!

16 September

The Little Elves

There was once a small village which was so peaceful and always happy. And, why? Because, each night, little elves came out to do everyone's work! The baker, who'd had to get up in the middle of the night, now slept beside his mixing bowls. The elves made the pies and the bread, kneading the dough and loading the ovens, making sure that every loaf was perfect.

And do you know what else they did to help the villagers?

17 September

Once, the butcher had to salt the hams and cut up the chops. Now, the elves did his jobs in the night, whilst he had a rest.

As for the carpenter, he was always giving them jobs to do! What did it matter, after all? The elves always got through the work!

When the wine merchant fell asleep, his wine was bottled by the time he woke up. And the kind little elves also thought of the mothers who were always so busy with household jobs that they never had any rest. The washing was done. They did the mending and the ironing.

And when the little tailor fell sick, the suits of clothes on which he had been working were finished by the next morning.

18 September

But the tailor's wife was a most bad-tempered woman, who hardly ever gave anyone more than a few minutes peace from her sharp tongue.

She thought that the elves were making her husband lazy. So, one evening, she waited for them to arrive, and chased them away with great thumps of her big broom.

The elves decided to go and help the people of another village! And, by the end of the next day, everyone discovered that they had to do all their own work, once again.

19 September

Timmy on the Trail!

Everywhere looks so lovely in autumn, with the most beautiful of colours.... red, yellow and brown, as well as green, which we can always see, whatever the season.

It's a good idea to make the most of the days when the last of the sunshine brings us dry, fine weather, by going out and looking around us – perhaps making a collection of the many different coloured leaves, too.

Andrew always gets his Dad to set up a tracking game for him and his friends.

But instead of chalking arrows to follow, he uses little bits of meat for Timmy, the dog, to sniff out, with Andrew holding his lead and everyone else close behind!

20 September

Andrew and Timmy always enjoy themselves! Timmy usually wants to follow all the wild animals and go along the forest paths like the rangers.

One day, Timmy led everyone along a track which became more and more difficult, going so fast that even Andrew could hardly keep up.

Perhaps he had made some sort of discovery, Andrew and his friends wondered? Could it be his Dad, hiding with the picnic he had promised?

It was a family of deer! Andrew could hardly wait to tell his father!

The Cry of the Oak Tree

One autumn day, an old oak tree was complaining to his neighbour, the fir tree. "What do I look like, now? The wind is blowing down all my leaves!" "They will return when spring comes!" the fir tree reminded him. "Yes," said the oak, "and I'll get so cold while I'm waiting! Nature is very cruel!"

"Well," the fir tree said, "I never lose my needles! Yet the winter does not spare me these hard frosts!"

"I know," sighed the oak tree. "But I still feel sad each year. Now, I'm going to sleep to try to forget my great unhappiness."

At this moment, the wind blew a lovely warm gust of air over the old tree. "Take heart, old tree!" said the wind.

21 September

22 September

The Oak Tree and the Reed

A magnificent oak tree lived alone in a meadow.

Nearby, a reed had put down roots by the river, and the oak tree was very fond of reminding the weed of his own strength and his importance.

"I think you should complain to Mother Nature!" the oak tree was always saying. "Why, a fine drizzle is a heavy load for you! And at the least bit of wind, just enough to ripple the surface of the water, you have to lower your head!"

"Why," the oak tree continued, "not only can I stop the rays of the sun itself, I can also brave the fiercest storm. If you did not have the shade from my leaves, I do not think you would last long at all!"

23 September

"And you live on wet ground where there is a lot of mist!" the oak finished by saying.

"I know I am thin," said the reed, "I bend – and yet, I never break, do I?"

But just a few days later, there was a hurricane force wind, strong enough to blow down everything in its path.

And the oak tree, so mighty and so proud, was finally beaten, uprooted, wrenched out of the ground.

The thin, little reed however, who could only bend with the wind, came through without any damage at all.

24 September

Plum Jam

Miss Ellis at the village school said she wanted to teach her class how to make jam.

"There are lots of plums in my Daddy's orchard!" cried Angela. "He wouldn't mind us picking some!"

"That is most kind, Angela!" smiled Miss Ellis.

And, in just a short time, Angela's class-mates were standing around the plum tree, looking up at the fruit which dangled down from above.

25 September

"Only pick the plums which are ripe!" said Miss Ellis. "They're the sweetest!" But the wasps soon began buzzing angrily. They did not like being disturbed by the children!
"Come along!" called Miss Ellis calmly. "I think we'd better go!" It was when they were all in the classroom once more that Miss Ellis noticed Wayne pulling a face.
"What's wrong, dear?" she asked.
"I've been stung," he groaned, going very red. "And in a very awkward place, too!"

26 September

Nutty the Squirrel

"Hello, my friends!" said a voice. "I'm Nutty the Squirrel!"
"And I'm Annette," said a little girl in surprise. "This is my brother, Jason. You look very busy."
"I'm storing up food for the winter," chattered Nutty the Squirrel. "And I must be quick about it! Lots of animals are doing the same, and if I don't hurry, there will be no nuts, acorns or anything!"
"Then why don't we help you?" said Jason. Annette nodded her head.

27 **September**

"Thank you!" said Nutty, very pleased. "All the fruit and nuts that you find, I'll put in my hidey-hole."

The two children were soon busy.

"Thank you for your help," murmured Nutty, looking around. "Now... where was I hiding my food?"

"There!" said Annette, pointing to a hollow tree.

"Really?" wondered Nutty. "I thought it was behind the flower beds...."

"No, Nutty!" laughed Jason. "It's where Annette told you!"

Nutty still looked confused. "I must be losing my memory!" he said.

28 **September**

The Mushroom Field

"Going to pick mushrooms, are you?" called out Mr. Green, the farmer, to Neil and Jane. "The fields are full of them, right now! I'll come and point out the best places and show you the ones you can pick and those which are best left alone."

And, shortly afterwards, Neil and Jane were on their way, both of them glad that they were wearing waterproof boots because it was very damp.

29 September

They soon found that Mr. Green was right. With each step, so it seemed, they found a mushroom! But what nobody told them, was that at the edge of the field, Daisy, the cow, was watching them.

Suddenly, she came closer, breathing noisily against Neil's neck. This frightened him so much that he began running as fast as he could!

In his haste, he tripped over and fell down, spilling the whole basket of mushrooms all over the ground.

But Daisy, the cow, just looked on. She did not like mushrooms, anyway!

30 September

The First Telephone Call

Tom is three years old today! More than anything else, he loves playing with the telephone. Mummy and Daddy keep telling him that it is not a toy.

But, for his birthday, they have said that Tom can make his first telephone call to Grandma and Grandpa. Mummy tells him the numbers to dial – and Tom is so pleased when Grandma's voice comes on the line! "Hello, Grandma!" he says proudly. "It's Tom here!"

1 October

The Sleeping Beauty

What rejoicing there was in a far-off kingdom, when the queen gave birth to a beautiful baby daughter! The king invited all the fairies to the palace to celebrate, so that they could cast good spells for the little princess.

But he forgot to invite one of them, and she marched into the royal chamber in a great fury! She said, that on her sixteenth birthday, the princess would prick her finger on a spindle and die! At once the king ordered all spindles in the realm to be destroyed. And one good fairy managed to alter the wicked spell, so that if the princess should prick her finger, she would not die, but go to sleep for one hundred years. And so the princess grew up, wise and beautiful.

2 October

In time, the wicked fairy's evil spell was forgotten. But, on her sixteenth birthday, the princess found a little door leading into a room, where an old woman sat at a spinning wheel. The princess drew near and touched the spindle! It pricked her finger, and at once she fell into a deep, deep sleep. Everyone else in the palace fell asleep, too, no matter what they were doing! Only the grass, the plants and the bushes did not sleep, and over the years, everything grew so tall and so thick, that the palace was hidden by a high, prickly thicket.

3 October

One hundred years passed. Then, one fine day, a handsome young prince, who was out riding, noticed the strange-looking wall of brambles and decided to take a closer look. At once, the green thorns and the creepers parted, so that he could make his way to the palace. Soon, he found the sleeping princess, thinking her so beautiful that he could not help kissing her. At once, she awoke. And everyone else in the palace awoke with her. And soon after, the beautiful princess married her handsome young prince.

4 October

The Story of the Nut-Shell!

Grandma was telling a story to her grand-daughter, Barbara.
"Do you know the one about the little worm who was so cold in autumn?" she said. "The snail helped him to make a tiny house from a nut-shell!"
"What a clever little thing!" thought Barbara. "I'd never have thought of using a nut-shell like that!"
"Oh, there are lots of things you can do with them!" smiled her Grandma.

5 October

Next time Barbara went to see her Grandma, there was a bowl of nuts on the table, with some nut-crackers, glue, paper and scissors – everything to make some nut-shell toys!
Remembering the story of the little worm, Barbara decided to make a nut-shell tortoise.
"I'll make some mice from my shells!" Grandma decided. "With a marble under each one, they can even move around!"
A thimble-case, a ship with a paper sail.... there were so many things to be made from nut-shells! Barbara and Grandma were busy all afternoon!

6 October

The Hunt is On!

Bang! Bang! Bang!
It was impossible for Benjy Bunny to put even his nose outside the warren, because of all the shots whizzing around!
All he could do was to hide down at the very bottom of the hole. Suddenly, the earth began to tremble above him, then a dog began barking. "I'll have to dig to get into the next rabbit warren!" he thought.

7 October

It was hard work. But at last, Benjy dug his way into the home of Hare, which was just a hole in the ground.
"Well!" cried Hare. "You might at least have come through the door!"
"The hunt is on, Mr. Hare!" Benjy panted. "The dogs are after me!"
"Don't worry, my friend," Hare said. "Follow me!" And he led Benjy into the sheltered hollow of an old tree.
"Close up the hole behind you!" he reminded Benjy. "Before long, we'll be in Malcolm's garden, somewhere those hunters will not be able to track us down!"

8 October

The Pillow Fight!

Do you know what Douglas and Giles like to do every morning, almost as soon as they wake up?
That's right! They have a pillow fight!
Then one morning, Giles stepped back and knocked down his new bedside lamp.
Their Mum was very angry, when she came into the room to see what all the noise was about.
"Right!" she said, "No pillow fights from now on!"

9 October

"Never mind!" whispered Douglas. "As soon as we're washed and dressed, we'll get some dustbin bags from the cupboard."

Giles was rather puzzled. "I can't see why you want dustbin bags," he said, "but, all right!"

Soon, the two boys were outside.

"Hurry up!" cried Douglas. "We can play out here, can't we? Let's fill up the dustbin bags with dead leaves, then we can have our pillow fight, just the same!"

Then Giles smiled again. Autumn, it seemed, had given them a new game!

10 October

Which Trees? Which Colours?

Now, autumn is well and truly here, and the whole of nature is getting ready for a long, winter sleep.

In school, Mrs. Baxter sat at a table, sorting through photographs which she had taken during the summer.

"Look at these trees!" she said to her children. "Can you tell me what they remind you of?"

They all studied them carefully, frowning in concentration as they put their imaginations to work.

11 October

"Well," said Luke at last, "the horse-chestnut reminds me of the colour of John's hair!" Everyone laughed.
"And the weeping willow is like a water fountain," said Mary, rather dreamily, "with spikes like emeralds in a casket lined with yellow silk!"
"That sounds good, Mary!" breathed Frances. "How did you think of it all?"
"I read it in a book!" laughed Mary. "They're very useful things you know!"
"It's a good way of learning," smiled Mrs. Baxter. "And without even leaving your house!"

12 October

Which Chestnut is Which?

What is the difference between the horse-chestnut and chestnuts? Both of them burst out of a prickly case, but the ordinary chestnut is smaller than the horse-chestnut, or "conker" as many of us call it. Nobody can eat conkers, but many animals love chestnuts, especially the squirrels. Have you ever tasted hot, roasted chestnuts? In winter, there are often people selling them in the streets. "Hot chestnuts!" they cry. "Hot, roasted chestnuts!"

The Swallows

Leaves begin turning yellow and the days become shorter when autumn arrives. Then it is time for Zip, the swallow, to fly south towards Africa, to spend the colder days of our winter in the warmer countries.

Swallows like Zip fly thousands of miles each year. It is quite a distance. And the nests, which the swallows always build in the corner of Anita's window frame, will still be there when they return in the spring.

But until the warmer weather returns again, everyone has to say farewell to the swallows and wish them a safe journey.

Did you know that when swallows nest under a roof or beneath a window, it brings good luck to the house?

13 October

It's Best to Leave in Good Time!

Anthony is rather a greedy boy. Every morning, before leaving for school, he gets himself some bread and butter, packets of biscuits, lots of fruit and puts it all in his big lunch box. One morning, he was longer than usual in the kitchen.

"Hurry up, Anthony!" his mother cried out. "You will have to run if you don't want to be late for school!"

Seeing the time, Anthony began running as fast as his legs could carry him, taking a short cut through the park for speed. And that was where he tripped up on a big stone!

Everything spilled out of his school bag, and without looking or stopping to think, Anthony just crammed the food back inside his lunch box!

14 October

15 October

Anthony just managed to get to school in time! But, because he was so greedy, he could not wait until play-time for something to eat.

Looking down at his school bag, he was amazed to see that it was moving! All eyes turned to see where the funny rustling noise was coming from!

"A mouse!" cried Anthony in amazement. "How did it get inside my lunch box? It's nibbling all my food!" How his friends laughed!

"It must have been when I fell over on my way to school," he told them. "Next time, I'll leave a bit earlier!"

16 October

Birds who Migrate

It was the first winter journey for Squawky, the stork. Everything was ready and her feathers smoothed down to help her get through the long flight.

"If you feel tired," said Squawky's mother, "just let me know! Then you can hold on to my wings for a while!" But Squawky had already made up her mind that she was not going to drag behind! No, she was already seeing herself as being at the very front of the line of storks!

17 October

What beautiful sights there were! "I shall have lots to talk about!" thought Squawky. But soon after, a dreadful thunderstorm broke out. Squawky was very frightened as she sheltered under her mother's wing. Then there was the snow, making it difficult for the birds to see their way. And, after being carried along by a whirlwind, it was lucky there was a big ship far below to lead the way and keep the storks together. Squawky knew now that she would have to fly many more long journeys before she could even think of leading the flight.

18 October

The Ugly Duckling

Mother Duck was very proud of her babies. Every morning, she would take them down to the pond. There she taught them to dive and swim, to hunt for worms and the other food they needed, and to defend themselves against their enemies, so that they would grow up to be good, strong ducks.

She had hatched five eggs, watching over them by night and by day, and now she watched the ducklings growing up around her.

19 October

But she was very sad at the sight of one of the ducklings, which was not at all like the others. He ate more because he was bigger, but he did not walk so well. In one month, there was no doubt about it – he was ugly!

And in another month's time, the ugly duckling, knowing how different he was to all the others, set off on his own, whilst Mother Duck slept.

On his way through the woods and forests, he met lots of birds. Some of them were shot by hunters, who also tried to kill him. Life was very hard, he thought, sitting alone on a river bank and watching some beautiful swans flying off somewhere warmer.

Winter arrived, the river froze, snow covered the earth and the ugly duckling could hardly find anything to eat.

20 October

Sad and hungry, the ugly duckling left the river and began walking. At last, he came to a little house, falling asleep at the door.

When he awoke, he found himself on a rug in front of a warm fire, with a dish of seed! He had been rescued by the old woman who lived there.

As spring returned, he went back to the river. And, as he bent his head to drink the water, he saw the reflection of the most beautiful white bird! The ugly duckling had become a magnificent swan!

21 October

The Giddy Chestnut!

What a wind! The leaves whirled around joyfully.

But Pico, the round, shiny, little horse-chestnut, just wanted to hide inside his prickly green case! Being so high up in the horse-chestnut tree made him feel giddy! All his friends had fallen already. But he was very frightened. He did not want to be made into a funny little animal, with four legs made of dead matchsticks!

"I wish I had some arms," he thought, trying to hold on, "or propellers would be even better. Then I could fly away and land gently in a nice, soft field....."

Just then, a gust of wind shook the branch and sent the little horse-chestnut tumbling to the ground. Now, what would happen?

22 October

Plonk! Pico felt himself rolling on the ground. But his fall was not as hard as he expected. Alan, sweeping up the leaves, heard him rolling around.

"This is a nice conker," he thought. "If I put it in the ground, it will grow into a lovely tree!"

He went to fetch a trowel, ready to dig a hole and put Pico inside.

"You are very kind," said Pico. "And I promise that I shall become as big a horse-chestnut tree as those you see near your school."

"That's if," added Pico, "you don't mind waiting a few years....."

23 October

A Walk in the Forest

The junior classes at school were going for a walk in the forest.
"Here are some nuts!" said Mr. Davis. "And look, there's a horse-chestnut tree, and an ordinary chestnut tree. Who can tell me which nuts taste the best?"
"Horse-chestnuts!" cried Isabel at once.
"No!" shouted Sara. "Ordinary chestnuts!"
"Let's try the two!" suggested Mr. Davis. "Gather up a few whilst I build a fire!"
And he got busy, arranging some dried grass and dead branches in the middle of a circle of big stones. Then, he lit a match.

24 October

The children put the two sorts of chestnuts in separate piles. Mr. Davis slit the shells of the ordinary chestnut. "To stop them going off bang while they are cooking!" he explained.
And he laid the chestnuts and the horse-chestnuts on the hot stones.
The children who tasted the ordinary, hot chestnuts really liked them!
But those biting into the horse-chestnuts? What faces they pulled!
"So everyone is agreed!" smiled Mr. Davis, throwing the empty shells into the fire, then making quite sure it was out before they went on their way.

25 October

Miga and the Butterfly

Miga, the spider, was all of a bustle! She had felt the first signs of frost, telling her she had to get ready for winter. So, at dawn, she wove her web between two stalks of a bush.

"Perhaps a moth or even a wasp will come this way," she thought. "And I must keep up my strength!"

But because of the fine drops of dew sparkling on the threads, all the insects could see the web very easily. Then, suddenly, along came a butterfly in search of some flowers, fluttering and looking around without taking too much care.... and in it flew, into the web! Miga the spider could not believe her luck!

Then, she stopped, seeing the butterfly beginning to struggle.

26 October

"You have such beautiful wings!" Miga could not help saying. "Like the petals of a flower!"

"P-please, Madame Spider," whimpered the butterfly, "please, have pity on a poor, lost butterfly!"

"But I'm so hungry!" said Miga.

"But my wings will not feed you!" cried the butterfly. "Please! Please, spare me!"

"Very well," said the spider at last. "It is not much to do for you."

And very gently, Miga freed the butterfly, taking care not to bruise its wings.

27 October

High Up in a Tree

Lydia and Vincent have an uncle who loves watching animals and birds. All through the year, he goes out into the forest and spends the whole day there. One day, he showed the children how to make an observation platform in a tree – and it was not long before Lydia and Vincent had made one, all by themselves!

It felt quite frightening, being so high up, when they had finished. They had needed lots of fallen branches, a good deal of patience and plenty of hard work. But what a splendid result! Their uncle promised that they could use it for the first time next day – as long as they were up early with a packed lunch to eat!

28 October

Next day, they did not have to wait long before Vincent saw a deer. "Look, Lydia!" he whispered. "It's coming ever so near."

"Can you give me something to eat?" she whispered back. I'm starving!"

But, Vincent dropped the picnic hamper. It was impossible to go and get it without frightening the deer! And before Lydia could say a word, a whole family of rabbits scampered along to enjoy this surprise feast! Lydia would have to wait for her lunch. The rabbits were enjoying it too much!

29 October

The Wolf and the Stork

There was once a wolf who felt so hungry, he gulped down all his food as though his life depended on it. No wonder he had a chicken bone stuck in his throat!

Luckily for him, a stork who happened to be passing nearby, heard his shrieks of pain, and she stopped, always ready to help wherever she could.

Just one look was enough for her to guess what had happened.

At once, without saying a word or wasting any time, she set to work. It was going to be a very long and a very difficult job.

But how could the stork help the greedy wolf?

30 October

At last, with the aid of her long beak, she got hold of the bone and pulled it out of the wolf's throat.

Now, any other animal would have been glad to pay the stork for what she did. And, when the wolf began walking away, without even thanking her, she said as much.

"You think I would pay you?" cried the wolf, finding his voice. "After digging into my throat with your long beak? You should be glad I don't eat you, you ungrateful bird! Go away, and don't get under my paws again!"

31 October

The Greedy Mouse

Little Mouse and Milly, the cat, were very good friends and they lived together on Mr. Brownlow's farm. And one day, after Little Mouse had told Milly all about the goodies in the cellar, the cat decided that she would also go down next time. "The store cupboard's in the far corner!" said Little Mouse. "I've already started work on the wire mesh!"

"We'd best hurry, then!" mewed Milly. "I can hear the farmer!"

Little Mouse could get inside the store cupboard through the hole she had made. Soon, she was tucking into the cheese, not forgetting to give some to Milly, the cat!

What a feast they had, eating first more cheese, then some sausage, enjoying themselves so much, it was some time before they heard the sound of footsteps on the stairs.

"Farmer Brownlow!" squeaked Milly. "Heaven help us!"

But Little Mouse had eaten so much that she could not get back through the hole, and the farmer was getting nearer every minute!

In the end, Milly knocked the store cupboard to the ground and it broke open so that Little Mouse could escape. But the two rascals were so frightened by what happened, that it was a long time before they went near the cellar again!

1 November

Snow-White and Rose-Red

There were once two sisters who lived with their mother in the country. One had brown-red hair, so they called her Rose-Red. The other, who was fair-haired, was called Snow-White.

One evening, after snow had covered the whole country in a white blanket, they heard knocking at the door – and there stood a magnificent brown bear, stiff with cold. They brought him inside and sat him in front of the fire.

And so he spent the rest of the winter with them, leaving with great sadness when the springtime came.

Then, one day in the summer, the two girls came across a dwarf with a long, fair beard.

2 November

The dwarf was struggling with a huge eagle who was trying to carry him off. Together, the two sisters hit out at the great bird, until it took flight. The dwarf did not even thank them. A little later, they met the dwarf again, this time with his beard caught in the wire of his fishing rod. But when the girls freed him, the dwarf only spoke rudely to them. And when they found him next day with his beard caught in the branches of a tree, the girls did not hesitate about cutting it to set him free, although he was just as rude.

3 November

ust then, their friend, the brown bear ame out of the bushes and gave the ngrateful dwarf a good smack!
hen suddenly, the bear changed into handsome young prince, and the ad-tempered dwarf changed into a ig stone.
he prince told the two sisters that he ad been under an evil spell cast upon im by the dwarf. Now, thanks to the elp of Rose-Red and Snow-White, the pell had been broken.
Rose-Red became the wife of the andsome young prince, and Snow-White married his brother.

4 November

A New Friend

"May I introduce Oliver!" Mr. Brown announced to his class. "He and his family have just moved here."
"Now," Mr. Brown went on, looking around the room, "is there a place for him, anywhere?"
"Here, sir!" cried Thomas.
"Perfect!" smiled Mr. Brown. "Anna, get an exercise book from the cupboard to give to our new friend, will you? Then we shall get on with our lesson!"

5 November

During the lesson, Mr. Brown kept an eye on Oliver's work.

"You're very good at arithmetic," he said, reading everything through at the end of the morning. "But I think you could do with one or two extra sessions in grammar. Would anyone like to help Oliver with this?"

Much to everyone's surprise, James put up his hand – a hand which was shaking slightly.

"The class is surprised," thought Mr. Brown, "but I am not. James is quiet and shy, but he is always there when anyone needs help. Well done, James!"

6 November

Room for Two!

Frisky, the squirrel, was looking for somewhere to spend the winter, but all the best places had already gone.

"I shall die from cold," thought the poor little squirrel, "if I do not find shelter before winter sets in!"

"Come and share my home!" offered Nutty in her sweet voice. "There's plenty of room for two, you know!"

And so the two squirrels spent the winter safe and warm and with plenty of food to last them until the spring came again.

7 November

A Pea-Souper

It was a very cold night – or, to be more exact, very "raw". Philip snuggled down in bed, as he usually did, but it seemed to take ages to get warm. And even when he went to sleep, his feet were still cold.

Next morning – what a surprise he had when he woke up!

"What on earth has happened?" he thought, going to the window. "I can't see a thing outside! Where are the trees?"

Even the pond had disappeared! Philip was still wondering about it as he went downstairs to have breakfast with his Mum and Dad. He was very confused about the mysterious blanket which seemed to have come down all around his home.

He went out into the garden.....

8 November

"I can't go far today!" thought Philip. "I can hardly see my own feet!" And he went back into the house to ask his father about it.

"Don't worry, son!" said his Dad. "It's only a thick mist which came down during the night. Do you know what a mist is? The house as well as the whole countryside is bathed in a sort of cloud. If you could look just two paces in front, you would see that it is made up of very fine drops of moisture suspended in the air. Just be patient. In a few hours, the sun will come and the mist will disappear!"

9 November

Things from Shoe-Boxes!

Whenever anyone buys a new pair of shoes in Donald's family, they always ask the shop assistant for the box! Everybody knows that Donald will always be glad to get some shoe-boxes – it's amazing the number of lovely things he can make with them! He puts everything he needs on the table before he starts work – poster paints, gummed paper, cardboard toilet rolls, odd beads, glue, scissors.... Donald collects so many things that sometimes he does not know where to begin. He always has so many ideas! So, what will be the first thing that he will make?
Try and have a guess!

10 November

Well, the first thing Donald makes with one of the shoe boxes is a splendid tunnel for his little brother's wooden train set. The second box is going to be something for Marie. Covered with some pretty paper and trimmed with ribbon, it will make a lovely doll's bed. Then he plans to make a garage for his brother's little cars.
Donald has already made his mother a lovely fruit basket.
He is always so busy during the long, winter evenings, that he never has time to get bored!

11 November

The Fox and the Stork

One lovely morning, Mr. Fox was thinking that he should invite his neighbour, Miss Stork, to supper.
He did not usually eat very much. So on this particular day, he only made a thin broth, ready to spoon out on to the little soup plates.
Poor Miss Stork! With her long, thin beak, she could not get one single drop!
Not like Mr. Fox – he managed to eat his meal, almost in a single instant!
Miss Stork thought this was very rude. So, to get her own back, she invited him to her home. And, Mr. Fox arrived right on time!

12 November

Such a lovely smell was coming from the kitchen. The most delicious-looking meat was served, cut up into little pieces.
But instead of plates, Miss Stork served it in vases with long, narrow necks. Her beak went in easily, but because Mr. Fox's nose was so much fatter, he could not reach the food.
Shamefaced, he went back home with an empty stomach, tail between his legs, ears drooping – and thinking of the saying:-
'Treat others as you would like them to treat you.'

13 November

What's Missing?

"What's this?" cried Dad. "No more milk in the 'fridge! Now, that's very strange... It doesn't seem all that long since I opened a bottle!"

"And who's had my washing basket?" Mum wondered, getting everything ready for the weekly wash.

"Has anyone seen my cardigan?" cried Grandma from the sitting room armchair, where she liked to sit.

"What's happened to the pillow on my bed?" cried Bruno.

It really was amazing, the number of things which seemed to be missing! Something's going on here!" said Dad. "We'll have to get to the bottom of it all. Now, where's little Caroline?"

Bruno looked all over the house, determined to find his little sister!

14 November

Bruno knew Caroline only too well, and he was fairly sure that if anyone knew what had happened to all the things which were missing, it would be her!

Just then, he heard her voice, coming from inside the garage. And inside, he could see his sister crouched over the washing basket. "What are you doing there, Caroline?" he asked her.

"Look, Bruno!" she smiled. "I couldn't leave this poor hedgehog out in the cold, could I? So, I brought him in from the side of the road, to stay with us for the winter!"

15 November

Such Travellers!

Not all the birds migrate when winter comes.
Instead of flying off to the warmer climates of other countries, they stay to face the cold weather of Europe.
How Speckley, the sparrow, envied the larger birds, such as storks, cranes and geese which he saw flying overhead.
"I'm sure I could do it," he thought, "with a friend to come with me." And he went off to find Fulton, the finch.
"Good idea!" said Fulton when Speckley told him. "All we need to do is follow the next flight of wild ducks!"
And so the two friends kept watch, until they caught sight of the ducks. Then, off they went, trailing after them, on their way to new adventures!

16 November

After two hours of flying, Speckley and Fulton were worn out.
"I – I can't feel my wings!" groaned Fulton.
"Do you think we shall get there soon?" puffed Speckley.
In the end, they decided to take a break and have a rest in a garden.
But the wild ducks went on their way with all speed, still flying as strongly as ever!
"Perhaps," said Fulton, "we are expecting too much to follow the larger birds. Let's go back to our own field, before we lose our way."

17 November

Pinocchio

There was once an old clockmaker called Geppetto. He had no family and lived quite alone. And after a hard day's work, he liked nothing better than making puppets from wood.

One night, a good fairy decided to reward him for his hard work, and made one of the puppets into a real, little boy! Full of joy, Geppetto gave him the name of Pinocchio, and put his name down for the best school in town.

Alas! Pinocchio could not have cared less about studying and learning! He was soon lured away by two rascals he met on the way to school.

Very soon, he found himself a prisoner, made to perform in a puppet theatre every night, and kept chained up when he wasn't on stage!

18 November

Pinocchio was soon sorry that he had not gone to school. He called on the good fairy for help, but even though she asked him to tell her the whole truth about what had happened, Pinocchio was soon making up stories. But, the more lies he told, the longer his wooden nose became!

At last, the good fairy thought Pinocchio had learned his lesson. Not only did she make his nose go back to normal, she also helped him escape. But Geppetto, full of sadness without Pinocchio, had locked up his house and gone in search of him.

19 November

Poor Geppetto had been swallowed by a great, big whale! And Pinocchio, thinking of all the heartache and misery he had brought to the old clockmaker, decided to save him and dived into the sea!
He was also swallowed by a whale – the same whale who had swallowed Geppetto! Together, they lit a big fire, which gave the whale such a bad tummy ache, he coughed up Geppetto and Pinocchio. At last, they could escape and go back home! Geppetto took up his work again, and Pinocchio became a fine son to him.

20 November

The Camera Safari

Dominic, Gary and Sonia were out with their uncle, walking in the forest. When they got to a spring, they stopped, resting their rucksacks against some rocks. Anyone looking on might have thought they saw the butt of a rifle in Dominic's rucksack.....
The three children nibbled biscuits, then sat in silence in the forest, well hidden in some sewn-up blankets. They were waiting for the wild animals to come and drink at the stream.

21 November

Suddenly, they all began speaking in whispers. Could it be a squirrel, a rabbit, or a hare coming near?
None of them were right! In fact, it was a deer, ears pricked up, coming up to the water with light, graceful little leaps.
Without a sound, Dominic took aim, looked carefully – and click! He took the photograph!
"I am the fearless hunter of pictures," he said, "thanks to Dad's old camera!"
And he patted the shiny, brown case.

22 November

Beating the Cold!

Richard was up early this morning! He got dressed very quickly, and now he is out in the garden, busy with some hard work – and doing something rather strange.
With his Dad's big garden spade, he makes a deep ditch all around each of the young trees in the garden. And when the next-door neighbour wants to know what he is doing, Richard just says, "No time to explain! I'll tell you another day!" What on earth is going on inside his head?

23 November

What with all the noise he makes, his Mum soon comes to the window.

"What are you doing, Richard?" she calls.

"Looking after the plants and the young trees!" he tells her. "They said on television that it was going to snow, and they will die of cold. We've got to get them indoors in the warm before it comes."

His mother raises her hands in horror. It's always the same with Richard, she thinks! He means well – but, if only he would think a little, first!

24 November

Trees Instead of a Compass!

Out walking with his big brother one day, Roland got lost in a wood. His brother had said that the way home was to the north – and how he wished he had a compass to show him where north was! Then he saw moss had grown on the same spot on the trunks of all the trees.

"This must face north," he murmured. "So, if I go the way the moss faces, I must find my way back home!"

And, he did!

25 November

Tree Planting

Today is St. Catherine's Day – the day when, according to tradition, all trees put down roots. Mr. Elliott's class are going to see if that is true by planting three beech trees!

Nobody forgets to put in the stakes, otherwise the first gust of wind could easily uproot a tiny tree. Then comes a piece of fencing all around, to stop cats scratching at the thin bark.

The next thing to do is to put straw around the foot of the tree to keep the roots warm during the winter.

26 November

"I can't wait until the spring to see the buds and the leaves!" cries Helen. "How long will it take to grow into a full-size tree?" Patrick wants to know.

"Fifteen to twenty years, young man!" smiles Mr. Elliott.

"Well, that's no good!" Patrick bursts out. "We'll all be grown-up by then!"

"You will be grown-up," agrees Mr. Elliott, "but when you see children – perhaps your own children – playing around these trees, you will think "that was a good thing we did!" and be proud of yourselves!"

27 November

Gareth and the Rook

Gareth was out with his Dad one cold November day, when he heard a funny sort of croaking noise.
"Sounds like a rook!" he said. "But rooks usually fly high up in the trees...."
He soon found where the croaking sound was coming from. A young rook lay on the ground, trembling with fear.
"It must be hurt," thought Gareth, "hit by a car, perhaps, or attacked by another bird."
Gareth could see that the bird was unable to fly, its eyes looking up at him, seeming to be pleading for help.
"Don't worry!" Gareth told the bird. "Daddy and I will take you home!"
And, very carefully he took the bird in his hands.

28 November

Back home, Gareth put the injured rook in a shoe-box and it soon began to get stronger, greeting him each morning with a loud "Caw-Caw!"
"Hey, you can speak!" cried Gareth. "Do you think you could say my name? Ga-reth..... Ga-reth...."
He spent no end of time trying to get the rook to learn to speak. And, what do you think? In the end, it really DID say Gareth's name!
"Well," smiled Gareth, very pleased, "now you only have to call my name whenever you need help, and I'll come running!"

29 November

The Chestnut Seller

Every winter, Mr. Bernard sold hot chestnuts. Grown-ups and children alike were always glad to see him beside his warm burner full of lovely, hot chestnuts!

The one thing they were sorry about was that nobody ever saw him smile. But then, they told each other, didn't Mr. Bernard live all on his own, without any family? That was not always so very nice.

One day, a white blanket of snow lay everywhere, as Mr. Bernard left his home. He had a long way to walk before he got to the market place. All at once, the old man stopped. Were his eyes playing tricks? Or, did a mound of snow in front of him actually move?

30 November

Carefully, Mr. Bernard crept towards the little heap of snow. And – what was underneath? A tiny, little kitten, half dead with the cold!

Gently, Mr. Bernard brushed away the snow and picked up the poor, little thing. Then, holding the kitten close to him, he turned back towards home. And, what do you think? He began to smile! What a change the people saw in him next day!

And when they asked him, he told them about his new friend, the little cat. He would never be alone again!

1 December

The Skating Rink

The temperature on the weatherman's thermometer was very low – seven degrees below zero! But the children in the village were delighted!

Dressed in their warmest, thickest clothes, they went out and made a lovely skating rink on the common. Then they put on their skates, doing their best to push off on to the smooth, shining ice. Some kept to the outside, feet sliding all over the place. Others crouched down, arms to their sides. A few more, the "old hands" and the "champions", bent their knees and went around three times without even going near the edges!

Louis could even skate on one foot – much to the astonishment of the others! And what about little James? Would he be as clever, they wondered?

2 December

James took one step forward, and then crash! He lost his balance. How everyone laughed as his head hit the ice.

All except Louis, that is. He had heard the bang on the ice.

"Are you all right?" he asked the little boy. "Look, take my hanky. You'll have to dry your tears before they freeze over and make slides for the flies around here!" That made James laugh.

"Now," said Louis, leading him on to the ice. "I'll show you how to skate without falling over...."

3 December

A Winter's Dream

Deep in his winter's sleep, Horace, the hedgehog, was having the most wonderful dream. In front of him was a great, big basket full of beautiful, rosy apples – so many that he called his friend, Hetty, to share in the feast!

"If you eat just one of those apples," she told him, "you will turn into a caterpillar!"

Horace did not believe a word of this! And, as night fell in the dream, and he began feeling hungrier and hungrier, he kept thinking of the basket of apples.

"What if I do turn into a caterpillar?" he thought. "Those apples look delicious!" And with his tiny, little teeth, he ate a whole apple without stopping. Then he decided to go to sleep.

4 December

Horace did not know how long he slept. But he had a tummy ache when he awoke. "It will soon go," he told himself, "I've just eaten too much." But the tummy-ache did not go away. Horace could see he was losing all his prickles, his paws shrinking into a long, wriggly body!

"Don't say I'm turning into a caterpillar!" he cried.

The dream was so frightening that Horace woke up in a sweat. Then he saw his paws and his prickles and wiped his brow. Thank goodness, he thought, it had all been a dream!

5 December

A Birthday for the Twins!

Although Stuart and Miranda's birthday was just a few weeks before Christmas, their Mummy and Daddy always made sure that it was a special day.

On the morning of their birthday, the two children came downstairs, went into the living room – and what a surprise they got!

A pile of toys and sweets stood at either side of the fireplace – on the right for Miranda and on the left for Stuart!

The twins enjoyed unwrapping all their presents, as well as tasting the gingerbread men and the pink marzipan pigs Mummy had made!

Then Daddy took some photographs, while Mummy went to fetch a special birthday breakfast of fresh rolls and hot chocolate!

6 December

Stuart and Miranda were not too interested in eating breakfast – not when there were cards to open and new toys to play with!

The day passed so quickly, it came as quite a surprise when Mummy told them that it was time for bed.

Miranda and her brother glanced at each other. Then they each put a toy and some sweets on the mantlepiece. "That's to give to the children who don't have anything at Christmas!" Stuart said.

Their Mummy and Daddy said nothing. But they both felt very proud.

How Very Strange!

All Juliet's family and friends know that she never goes anywhere without her favourite, little, furry, brown bear. One day, however, this bear had quite an adventure.

It had been snowing heavily, and Juliet had been playing outside all day with her friends.

First they had built the most wonderful snowman, complete with an old, straw hat and a ragged shawl they had rescued from the loft.

Then they had gone up and down on their sledges, throwing snowballs and making slides.

But, when she got back home – what a shock for Juliet! She could not find Bumble, the brown bear!

7 December

8 December

"Don't worry, Juliet!" said her Daddy, giving her a hug. "We'll go out and look for Bumble tomorrow. We'll find him, don't you fret!"

Juliet had terrible nightmares that night!

But, next day, just as her Daddy had said, she found her little, brown, furry bear.

And, do you know where he was? In the arms of the snowman!

And from that day to this, nobody ever knew how Bumble got there.

Nobody except the snowman, that is....

A Tasty Treat

We do not always have to buy Christmas presents! So often, the nicest gifts are those which we make ourselves.

Each year, when Christmas is coming, Bruce and Elaine make chocolate truffles for their godmother.

And this year, today is "Truffle-Making Day"!

Mummy has put the ingredients on the kitchen table:–

200 grammes of cooking chocolate
60 grammes of butter
the yolk of an egg
4 dessert spoonfuls of icing sugar
4 dessert spoonfuls of cocoa
and some little paper cups to put the truffle mixture into.

Elaine has already decorated some boxes to put the truffles into, later on.

9 December

10 December

First, Mummy melts the butter over a low heat, then stirs in the rest of the ingredients. The mixture is allowed to get nice and cold in the fridge. Then comes the best part for Elaine and Bruce..... rolling it into little balls with their fingers!

"I can make mine nice and round!" grins Bruce.

"This one is too big!" says Elaine. "I'd better eat it!"

It's lucky Mummy is keeping an eye on them – just to make sure that there are enough chocolate truffles left for their godmother's Christmas present!

Has Life Stopped?

Now winter really has arrived. Everywhere is silent, and in the clear, frosty night, a big halo can be seen around the moon, and the sky is full of stars.

The wild animals have stored plenty of food, and, most important of all, have built a home to shelter them from the ice and snow. Most of us like being inside in the warm, rather than going out in the bitter weather, and it is the same with animals.

No wonder many of them, such as the hedgehog, decide to sleep away the winter months.

In fact, the whole countryside is slowly going to sleep, only waking again with the first rays of spring sunshine, three long months away.

11 December

12 December

The Horse and the Wolf

When it is springtime, horses leave their stables and spend more time out in the open.

That is when a hungry wolf roaming around chanced to see a lovely horse. But, as the horse was too big for the wolf to kill on his own, he decided to try and trick him, instead.

"My friend," he said, "I know all the flowers and plants in this meadow and the cures which these can work. If you ever have anything wrong with you, just tell me and I'll put you right!"

But the horse knew very well that the wolf was trying to trick him.

"As a matter of fact," he said, "there is a thorn under my shoe and it's very painful! Do you think you could help me?"

13 December

The wolf could not believe his luck! "Why, of course, my friend," he said, coming forward. "I'll soon have you feeling better!" And he bent down, pretending to have a look at the horse's hoof, and – wham! The horse gave that wolf such a blow, right on his hairy chin!

"It's true what they say," groaned the wolf, nursing his broken chin. "Everybody has their strong point. If only I had listened to my father and kept my mouth shut, I would never have had a taste of my own medicine!"

14 December

Good Wishes

Paddy, the postman, was always busy as Christmas time drew near. It seemed that he never stopped work, his post-bag full of Christmas cards. What's more, it was very cold, and the slippery pavements often made it difficult for him to get around.

And yet, he always had a smile for everyone, even though his fingers were frozen and his shoulders ached. "If only I could rest for a little while," he often thought to himself.

15 December

Then one day, just as he was thinking how nice it would be to have a break, he slipped on the pavement and fell! "Ouch!" he groaned. "I can't move my leg! I hope I haven't broken it!"
"I'm afraid your leg is broken," said the doctor at hospital.
And so, Paddy had to stay there. Having a rest would do him no harm, he knew. But now, he felt so alone. What Paddy did not know, then, was that when everyone heard about his accident, they all agreed to write him a letter. So, for once, there were some good wishes for him!

16 December

Madame Snow

There was once a lovely, little girl who lived with her step-mother and step-sister. One day, in the garden, she dropped a spindle in the well.
Reaching in to get it back, she fell into the well, and found herself in a huge garden.
She was astounded to see an enormous house and went towards it at once.
On the way, she saw an oven where rolls were cooking.

17 December

"Take us out!" they cried. "We are too hot!" And so, the girl did as she was asked.

Then an apple tree, heavy with fruit, called to her. "Will you shake my branches to bring some of these heavy apples tumbling down?" And so, the girl did as the apple tree asked.

Then, she knocked at the door of the house.

Madame Snow came out and asked the girl if she would help her with the housework. The girl agreed. And when all the work was done, she made her shake the eiderdown.

All at once, the country was covered with a fall of snow!

Madame Snow was very pleased and showed the girl how to get back home.

But, as she passed through the door, the girl saw that the pockets of her apron were filled with gold pieces.

18 December

When she got home and told her story, the girl's step-sister decided that she, too, would go and get herself some gold pieces – but without doing any work for them!

So, she went down the well and into the big garden.

But she would not help the rolls, nor the apple trees, nor Madame Snow with the housework. "Then, go back where you came from!" said Madame Snow. And as the girl passed through the door, the whole contents of a barrel of tar fell on her head!

19 December

The Key

"What's that?" said Alice, bending underneath the cupboard in the living room. "I thought I saw something shining..... It's a key!" she cried. "Now, where could that have come from? Maybe Julian will know where it belongs!" Julian shook his head. "No, I've never seen it before!" he said. "Do you think it could be the key to the cellar?"

"No, it's too small!" said Alice. "It looks more like the key to a cupboard."

"Maybe it's the key to the cupboard where Mummy hides the biscuits and sweets!" she went on. "Why don't we try it and see, while she's out at the shops? I wouldn't mind something nice to eat, would you?"

20 December

Alice and Julian searched all over the house. But the key fitted none of the cupboards. "There's only the little cubby-hole under the stairs left," sighed Julian. "That's our last hope!" They put the key in the lock – and, to their delight, it turned easily!

"I-I don't believe it...." breathed Alice as the door clicked open to reveal all the Christmas decorations, stored away for safe keeping!

"Let's put them up!" cried Alice. "Give Mummy a surprise when she gets back?"

21 December

Winter Weather!

To Robbie, the rabbit, it seemed the whole wood was covered by a great, big, white carpet!

Robbie was not yet three months old, so he had never seen snow before. He ran inside to Mother Rabbit, just as fast as he could.

"Mummy!" he cried. "I can't go out, because there's this great, big, white carpet over all the fields!"

"It snowed last night, that's all, Robbie!" smiled Mummy. "You can still play outside!"

"But it feels so cold," protested Robbie. "Can't you come with me?"

"I have to look after the house," his Mummy reminded him. "Why not go and ask Ralph rabbit, next door?" So, Robbie put on his woolly hat and a scarf.

22 December

In just a few leaps and bounds, Robbie was calling for Ralph at his home! "Make sure you keep well away from any sound of gun-shots!" said Ralph's Daddy. "Remember, you will be seen that much more easily against the white background, so stay close to the warren!"

But none of this worried the two friends! First, they had great fun with a snowball fight, then they built a huge rabbit of snow, with Ralph making big snowballs for Robbie to build the snow-rabbit's body!

23 December

Nearly Christmas!

The Christmas holiday has begun! "Crazy how time flies!" sighs Daddy, bringing in the Christmas tree. Brian and Helen have unpacked two boxes of fairy lights, as well as the Christmas tree garlands and glass baubles.

Daddy puts the tree on a low table, so that the lights will work better.

"You can put them on the tree," he tells the children. "Then we'll finish off by threading on the garlands and the baubles."

This is a job which Brian and Helen always enjoy very much! And, as well as decorating the tree, they like setting out the Christmas crib, too.

On Christmas Eve, 24th December, Mummy and Daddy will give a special present to Brian and Helen for helping at this busy time.

24 December

But it is Mummy and Daddy who have the surprise! When they have given their present to Brian and Helen, they get a gift, too!

"We hope you'll like it!" says Helen, giving them each a big hug.

"Because we love you!" adds Brian with a smile. And, when Mummy and Daddy take off the wrapping paper – it's a photograph, an enlargement of a family holiday snapshot!

"Thank you, my dears!" say Mummy and Daddy, both together.

"We said we hoped you'd like it!" laughs Brian.

25 December

Merry Christmas!

Mr. and Mrs. Edwards always invite their parents for Christmas dinner. And, whilst their Daddy is pouring out some wine for the grown-ups, Brian and Helen always help Mummy with the food.

"I like the pudding best!" says Helen. "Are you going to let us do the Christmas log?" Brian wants to know.

"All in good time," laughs Mummy.

It's a lovely Christmas dinner! First, here is the "starter" – crab salad on a lettuce leaf with slices of hard boiled egg. Then comes a dish of croutons to go with the vegetable soup.

The main dish is the family's favourite – roast turkey, with peas, brussel sprouts and roast potatoes!

"What a feast!" says Brian, after he and everyone else has cleared their plate. "Now, what about the Christmas log?"

"Here it is!" smiles Mummy, bringing the plate in. "Would you like to decorate it for us?"

"You know we would," laughs Helen. Brian loses no time in getting the cream out of the refrigerator, with Helen going to fetch the icing set.

"We'd better taste the cream," says Brian, "just in case it's turning a bit sour....."

"Best to make sure it's all right!" agrees Helen, licking her fingers.

"Don't forget to leave some to decorate the Christmas log!" smiles Mummy.

"Never mind," Helen whispers to her brother, "we'll have another helping at tea-time!"

26 December

Hansel and Gretel

There was once a poor wood-cutter who lived with his wife, and his son and daughter, Hansel and Gretel. Times were very hard, and there cam a day when there was nothing to eat. The wood-cutter had no choice but to take the children into the forest, in the hope that a rich nobleman out huntin would find them.

When they had gone as far as they could, the wood-cutter lit a fire, so tha the children could lie down and go to sleep. Then he went away.

Night had fallen when Hansel and Gretel awoke. They knew they could not find their way home in the dark! Next day, after walking for what seemed like a long, long time, they came across a pretty, little house.

27 December

Hansel and Gretel could see the roof of the house was made of chocolate, the walls of currant bread and the windows of white sugar! By now, they were very hungry indeed, so they each broke off a piece of currant bread. Just then, an old woman appeared on the door-step, offering them both food and shelter. Hansel and Gretel did not know it then, but she was a witch! She put Hansel in a cage, meaning to fatten him up to eat, and made Gretel do all the housework. Each morning, the witch would feel Hansel's finger, to see if he was getting any fatter.

28 December

Being very short-sighted, the witch could not see Hansel holding out a bone for her to feel, not his finger! Why was he still thin, she wondered? At last, she lost patience! Fat or thin, she said, she would eat Hansel. Gretel was told to build a fire and boil a huge cauldron of water. She asked the witch to test if it was hot enough – then crept up behind her and pushed her in! Hansel was rescued and soon they were safely back home, with treasures from the house in the forest to make sure they were never in want again.

29 December

Scampy is Hungry!

Scampy, the squirrel, had no food left! Now, he was searching around for something to eat!
"You are too greedy, young squirrel!" the old oak tree told him. "You'll find it's always best if you save a little!" "I won't be greedy again!" promised the little squirrel, close to tears.
"Then look under the big stone just here," said the oak tree after a pause. "I hid a few of my acorns there for silly little squirrels like you!"

30 December

The New Year's Eve Party

Appledale's little town hall is buzzing with excitement!

Each year, everyone is invited to a party for New Year's Eve, with fun and games, music and dancing for all the people, grown-ups and children.

But, things are rather different this year, because the Mayor has given the job of putting up the decorations to the children at the junior school. And how they all love helping with this most important task!

Anthony has been put in charge, and he is very well organised, making sure that everybody knows exactly what they are meant to be doing.

Suzanne's team has the job of putting up the garlands around the walls.

31 December

The youngest children have the job of sorting out all the false noses, the streamers, and the party hats.

When everyone comes into the hall, they see what the children have done.

"Wonderful!" cries the baker.

"A splendid job!" agrees the postman.

"Our congratulations!" adds the Head Teacher of their school.

"So, now the party can begin!" says the grocer, putting bottles and glasses on each table. "Let's drink to a Happy New Year for everyone!"

Index